Your Second Brain

And Why It Is The Key To Your Health, Success and Happiness

Leo Carter

Table of Contents

STOP!

YOU'RE PROBABLY GOING TO WANT TO READ THIS BEFORE GOING ANY FURTHER!

How would you like to enjoy our books for free?

And

Have influence on the creation of our books like covers, chapters and more…

Well you can and it's pretty simple, you can join our reader's circle and as well as get the benefits above you will get book recommendations, tips and advice from others in our amazing circle.

BRAIN ATHLETES

If you want to join our reader circle copy the link below into a web browser

https://bit.ly/READERSCIRCLE

A FREE GIFT!

As a thank you for purchasing this Book we have decided to give away a free gift. The gift we have decided to give is a 2 week meal plan which will heal and restore your gut and microbiome to optimal health.

This meal plan has a variety of tasty and easy to make recipes and I am confident you will love being on this diet. I and my team have personally engaged in this diet found the food to be delicious and the diet satisfying and easy to maintain.

Just copy the text below into a web browser

to get this guide

https://bit.ly/secondbrain2

BRAIN ATHLETES

We have also included 17 amazingly tasty recipes you can try.

Take action to a healthier, happier and tastier life.

Just copy the text below for our yummy meal plan!

https://bit.ly/secondbrain2

Introduction

Scientists are learning more about the "second brain."

Inside of you, you have what scientists call a "second brain." Of course, two heads are better than one, but that's not what we're referring to here. Instead, we're going to be exploring the powers of your enteric nervous system (ENS). Your "second brain" is the mesh of neurons located throughout your entire gastrointestinal tract - basically from your mouth through to your bowels. Since it can operate completely independent of our cerebral brain, and controls much more than simple digestion, it's referred to as the "second brain." In fact, some researchers refer to this plexus of neurons as the first brain, since it evolved prior to the central nervous system (CNS).

By reading this guide, you will learn that your gut can actually teach you about your other bodily systems, such as your cognitive function and weight fluctuation. When you learn how to listen to your gut, you will become much more aware of how you function as a whole. You will even have a better understanding of the way that your moods form and why you feel certain things more intensely.

Your "second brain," isn't a single entity, it's actually a multifunctional system in your body that should never be ignored. After understanding the way it works and why it is considered the "second brain," you'll see just how truly helpful it is to trust your gut instinct. Indeed, your "second brain," can send your brain signals and other hints that are necessary for remaining healthy and fully-functional - physically and emotionally.

As you read through the chapters in this book, you'll see how much your second brain is in control. It can influence nearly every part of your body, so it is important to treat it with the best care possible. What you put into your body is going to manifest into the fuel that keeps you going throughout the day. By having a clear understanding of the way that your gut works, you will be able to make the smartest choices for your optimal health.

Chapter 1: The Second Brain and the Microbiome

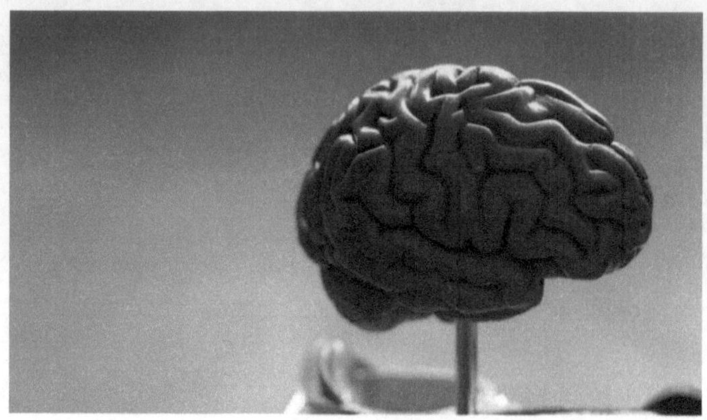

The relationship between your "first brain" and your "second brain" is slowly being understood.

There are millions of neurons within your gastrointestinal tract. Not only do these neurons control how to digest food - what to keep and store, and what to expel - the mouth, esophagus, stomach and intestines, or gastrointestinal tract, also sends signals to the brain that act as a sort of health report.

For example, your gut can pick up on nervous energy, so an indicator of anxiety. It can also recognize when harmful bacteria are moving in and making you sick. Once alerted of these presences, your gut will communicate with your brain via the neurons in an effort to protect your body.

Breaking it down, the enteric nervous system (ENS) is actually what is responsible for sending these signals to your brain. This system operates independently of the spinal cord and the brain, proving that it is a very powerful resource. It's easy to observe the way that the ENS generates energy in the colon, yet tracking its role with neuron production has proven to be more difficult. Through scientific research, it has been found that a certain pattern of activity is present in the ENS. Neurons could be seen firing repetitive bursts of energy to activate muscle cells at the same rate. This is how your second brain tells your body to keep the digestion process moving along.

Cooperation

While your ENS acts as another brain in your body, it can't tell you how to interact with other people or how to complete your tasks at work. Unlike your main brain, your ENS isn't responsible for your thinking. Instead, it maintains its role as the controller of your digestion and the helper of enzyme distribution. Jay Pasricha, M.D., director of Johns Hopkins Center for Neurogastroenterology, states that the ENS does communicate with the main brain and has the ability to create profound results.

Without cooperation between these two brains, your body would not be nearly as functional and protected. Emotionally, the ENS can actually help you by shifting your mood and your feelings. When you experience such problems as irritable bowel syndrome or constipation and diarrhea, it is normal to feel pain and bloating. Many doctors used to think that the presence of these problems is what causes anxiety and even depression, but they have come to find that it is actually the other way around.

Pasricha says that researchers are understanding evidence that states the irritated ENS might be sending signals to the central nervous system (CNS). In turn, this can trigger emotional mood changes that are felt by the individual. Through these findings, it is clearer as to why those who suffer from irritable bowel syndrome and other bowel-related problems are known to develop emotional problems such as anxiety and depression. This is very important research because around 30-40% of the population suffers from bowel-related problems at some point in their lives.

Since scientists can now identify the importance of the ENS-CNS connection, there are more treatment options available that take into account the emotional aspects of these ailments. Some examples include antidepressants, cognitive behavioral therapy, and medical hypnotherapy. Since the two brains regularly communicate, these treatment options become a way to effectively treat several problems at the same time. Even if a patient does not necessarily suffer from a mental illness, a gastroenterologist might still prescribe an antidepressant to aid with IBS because it will address both the intestinal discomfort and the mood attached.

There is still a lot of research to be done about the two brains and the ways in which they communicate. Some scientists believe that these communications can also be responsible for thinking skills and memory-related functions, as well. Admittedly, Pasricha states that this is an area that is still in need of some further research. It does open up an interesting idea, though. The gut is much more helpful than we even believed to be possible.

Another interesting idea is the way that the digestive system can signal the brain and inform it about metabolism and diabetes. This type of interaction involves the communication between the gut, nerve signals, and microbiota (the bacteria that live inside the digestive system). By learning about these health risks, an individual might be able to prevent them from worsening.

Bacteria

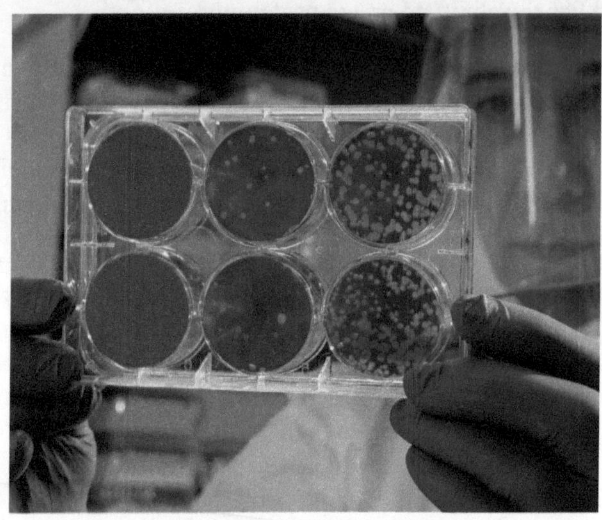

Scientists are uncovering more information about our gut microbiome.

Inside your body, at any given moment, lives bacteria that serve their own unique purpose. Certain bacteria can cause diseases and make you sick, but there are many exceptions. This "good" bacteria in your gut is known as the microbiome. It's counterintuitive to think that bacteria can be "good," but the gut microbiome is essential for keeping you healthy. It strengthens your immune system because, in a very real way, it functions as an additional organ. Most of these microbes live in your intestines and can be found in a large pocket where they are stored until they need to take action. Ironically, these microbes in your gut can weigh up to 2-5 lbs, similar to your brain.

Microbes are not a new development, of course. Humans have lived with them playing this crucial role throughout our existence. As soon as you are born, your gut microbiome is activated. As a baby passes through the mother's birth canal, this is known as one of the first encounters with microbes outside of the womb. The microbiome diversifies as you get older. It is thought that a higher microbiome is an indication of superior health. The food that you eat can affect the diversity of your microbiome.

These are some of the ways in which your microbiome can change the way your body operates:

- Breast Milk Digestion: Bacteria that are known as Bifidobacteria develop in babies' intestines. It helps them digest the healthy sugars in breast milk necessary for growth.
- Fiber Digestion: With bacteria to help you digest fiber, you will be able to fight off diseases such as diabetes, heart disease, and cancer.
- Immune System Control: The gut microbiome tells your immune system how to work. It can signify what to do in case of an infection.
- Brain Health: According to new research, the gut microbiome also has a hand in controlling brain function because of the way it communicates with the central nervous system.

When you have a rich selection of bacteria in your gut, this is going to successfully break down important nutrients that are necessary for feeling energized and strong. With these bacteria, you will be able to thrive both physically and mentally. Many people consume foods like yogurt, sauerkraut, kombucha and fermented cheeses that contain live cultures found in probiotics that are meant to create more good bacteria. Not only do these cultures aim to promote great digestive health, but they will also make sure that your body is protected.

If you are interested in improving your gut's microbiome diversity, you need to keep in mind that the food that you eat is the key. Work on consuming a wide range of whole foods. Some notable health foods for your gut are legumes, fruit, and beans that contain a lot of fiber and Bifidobacteria. Fermented foods, as mentioned above, like kefir are also great options. Make it a point to eliminate as many artificial sweeteners as you can because these stimulate unhealthy bacteria.

Chapter 2: How our Second Brain Controls Us Far More than we Realize

Like a video game, our second brain almost acts as a joystick for the rest of our health.

Thinking deeply about the second brain, you will begin to understand its total influence. Because it can communicate with your main brain, you will realize that a lot of information is being shared on a daily basis. Your second brain can identify how to respond to stress. As mentioned, the feeling in the pit of your stomach when you are surprised or scared comes from deep inside of your gut. When this happens, your gut microbiome is all communicating with your body, saying that it needs to respond in a certain way. Naturally, you can see how this might play a role in the development of stress-related illnesses such as anxiety and depression.

Scientists have explored these relationships through studies done on mice. After manipulating the gut bacteria in the test subjects, the mice are raised without exposure to outside air and contaminants in an effort to keep them as pure as possible. When the germ-free mice are placed in a maze, they spend a lot of time out in open areas and act unafraid of being there. The control mice tend to explore but resort to resting in closed-off areas as a form of protection. This seems to indicate that mice with lower levels of bad gut bacteria tend to feel less anxious and worried.

Considering the way that your gut can influence your mental health, you can also see how it can impact your social behavior. When you get a gut feeling while being around another person, this is going to change the way that you express yourself. If you are feeling judged by someone, you are probably going to present a quieter version of your personality and hold back more than you usually would. Alternatively, if you are comfortable, your gut is going to feel more relaxed and you are likely going to feel able to communicate and express yourself with ease.

If you have mood swings, you can see how this can potentially be connected to what you are eating and how healthy your gut is. The second brain is fueled directly by what you decide to put into your body. If you are loading up on artificial foods and preservatives, then you are going to feel lethargic and unwilling to do as much as you would if you were eating whole foods that nourished you. By changing your diet, you might discover that this is all it takes to regulate your moods and maintain a healthier general disposition.

Recent research has led scientists to the conclusion that changes in the gut microbiome can influence your risk of disease. Therefore, manipulation of the microbiome can provide brand new ways to intervene during cases of anxiety, depression, and other mood disorders. What used to be a solitary focus on the way that the brain operates has now left a lot of room for thinking and considering what the second brain can do in a situation like this. Because your gut microbiome can lead to behavioral changes, it makes sense that its manipulation would create an impact in the way that mental illness would develop or worsen.

The next time that you think your diet does not matter or relate to the way that you are feeling mentally, you will likely think again. Your gut health should now become a priority to you after discovering all that it can do and how it can make you feel. Your second brain is always communicating with your central nervous system, so you must do your part in making sure that it has what it needs in order to function properly. Consider that not all bacteria are bad bacteria, so you do not have to aim to have a stomach that is free of this. For a stable mood and a way to avoid dangerous illnesses, you need to have an enteric nervous system that is going to do its part to warn you when something is wrong.

Dopamine and Serotonin

Emotions are clearly tied to general health, including the health of our gut microbiome.

Think about your gut bacteria sending messages to your brain. It has its own type of delivery system that both produces and responds to dopamine, serotonin, melatonin, norepinephrine, and acetylcholine. As you probably know, your brain uses all of these chemicals to regulate your mood and to determine how you are going to function. When an army of bacteria is responsible for sending messages to your brain, it is likely to listen. Knowing that there is strength in numbers, your brain is going to want to remain aware of its actions and activities. How communication truly unfolds is still being researched, but from what scientists can see, the environment is extremely interactive.

To understand the communication that is taking place, it is helpful to understand the roles that both dopamine and serotonin play. Both are neurotransmitters that are known for helping your body function in several ways. They both affect your quality of sleep and the capacity of your memory. Physically, your metabolism is also impacted by these chemicals. As you can see, there are many ways in which your mood is going to be impacted if you have any kind of chemical imbalance in your brain. In order to keep both of your levels up, your brain needs to receive the proper signals to produce more.

The neurons in your brain release dopamine, which is meant to carry additional signals through your nervous system. With dopamine, your body is able to create norepinephrine and epinephrine. A critical part of your mental health, dopamine can also control your desire, cravings, and motivation. If you feel that your dopamine levels are fluctuating, this is likely a result of one of the following factors:

- Blood flow
- Sleep quality
- Mood

- Movement
- Alertness

Another neurotransmitter in your brain is serotonin. This is another feel-good chemical that your body needs in order to keep you feeling happy. More than 90% of your serotonin resides in your gut. This is what helps regulate the movement of your digestive system. As you can see, it is very important to listen to your second brain when it comes to creating enough serotonin to keep you functioning regularly. If your levels start to fluctuate, the following issues tend to show up:

- Mood problems
- Metabolism/Appetite
- Sleep quality declines
- Body temperature fluctuates (too hot or too cold)
- Hormonal imbalances
- Cognition/Concentration problems

While both chemicals are responsible for relaying messages, they do have their differences. Your dopamine levels are mainly responsible for body movements and coordination. It is also a component of your brain's pleasure and reward center. It is the driving force behind many of the behaviors that you do on a regular basis. The more dopamine you have in your system, the happier you will feel. Also, you will feel more motivated.

Serotonin is great at regulating your mood and can even impact your sexual desire. It is also linked to appetite/digestion and your sleeping habits. Overall, there is a lot that will change if you find that your serotonin levels are low. You can't have one chemical without the other, as both work in a balanced way to keep you happy and functional. When you don't have enough serotonin, this can lead to an overproduction of dopamine as your body's way of trying to stay balanced.

The two have opposite effects on your appetite, which can lead to changes in your gut health. Serotonin suppresses your appetite while dopamine activates it. When there is a chemical imbalance, you might be lacking the desire you need to eat the foods that your body craves. Your impulsivity is also controlled by these two chemicals. Serotonin limits your impulsivity, while dopamine promotes it. If you notice that you are acting out of the ordinary, this might be an indication that you aren't producing enough serotonin.

As you can see, if one of the two becomes overpowering, this can quickly change your mood, behavior, and digestive system. It is important to make an appointment with a doctor if you notice that you just aren't feeling as well as you used to. An imbalance is one of the main ways for anxiety and depression to develop, as well. It is best to get a handle on the situation before it presents itself as a bigger problem. Without you even realizing it, these chemicals are working hard inside of your body to present you with a guideline necessary to live your life. Listen to your instincts and make sure that you go for a check-up if something feels off.

Chapter 3: The Second Brain and Mood

Emotions are deeply affected by the second-brain, and vice versa.

Your mood can often be one thing that is hard to control. Many factors are involved that dictate how you are going to feel and how you are going to react as a result of your feelings. As you navigate through your life, you are going to experience many ups and downs. Accomplishments will build you up and challenges will test your strengths. The things that you do to make yourself feel better do not only have to be mental, as you now know how much the second brain can impact your mood. By having a complete understanding of the way that your stomach can change your mood, you will be able to stay healthy and do what is best for your mental health.

Influences

Because there are so many neurons in your enteric nervous system, you are actually able to feel the inside of your gut in more ways than one. Just as you are able to recognize hunger and stomach pain, you are also able to adapt to fear and anxiety. Most of what you feel on a daily basis can likely be attributed to your digestive system. The more you eat, the harder your digestive system works to break down all of the food. This process is mechanical and precise, something that you should be very familiar with at this point. If anything goes wrong during the digestion process, you are also able to feel this in the form of a stomach ache or nausea.

Part of what makes your gut so interesting is that it can work independently from your brain. With its own set of reflexes and reactions, your brain does not actually have to think about each step in the digestion process for your body to follow through with it. This allows your body to perform the task without having to rely on the spinal cord to send signals back and forth from the main brain. This is only a small highlight of the complexity of the second brain, though.

Emeran Mayer, professor of physiology, psychology, and biobehavioral sciences at UCLA, suggests that the second brain has evolved in a way that showcases it has more abilities than just assisting you with digestion. For example, 90% of the fibers in the vagus nerve (the primary visceral nerve) actually carry information from the gut to the brain (Hadhazy, 2010). In the past, it was thought that this would be the other way around. Your gut has a lot to say about your health and it is constantly communicating with your brain in an effort for it to stay on top of this.

Admittedly, scientists believe that our state of mind is determined in some obscure ways by our second brains. They believe that human emotions are greatly decided off of gut instincts. While there is no way of knowing for sure how much the second brain can control, clearly there is a distinct and powerful connection. An example of this is the feeling of having butterflies in your stomach. When you feel this way, you aren't just thinking about this as a physical sensation. It is usually paired with an emotional response, such as nerves or excitement.

When thinking about the bigger picture, your mental health can have a bigger impact on your stomach than you realize. For certain depression treatments, for example, your gut is being impacted unintentionally. For instance, because the enteric nervous system uses over 30 neurotransmitters, medications like SSRIs (selective serotonin reuptake inhibitors) increase serotonin levels and can leave you with an irritated stomach. Irritable bowel syndrome has also been found to be a common side effect.

Mental health issues that were formerly thought of as problems that reside exclusively in the brain are now being seen as a whole-body issue. It is important to look at the entire picture when treating these disorders because you never really know what side effects might be present when you fix one thing but not another. Keeping the entire mind and body balanced will always be the best method for feeling your best. This can prove to be very challenging when the gut is such a powerhouse of a system.

The things that you can do for yourself to protect your gut health are fairly simple. You do not need to ask your doctor for any medication unless you are suffering from a disorder such as irritable bowel syndrome or something comparable. On average, it just takes a little bit of care to ensure that you are paying close enough attention. As we discussed earlier, eating right is the main thing that is going to keep you feeling great. This can be defined differently for all, but it should be common sense to you based on what your body needs and craves. Your lifestyle is also going to be a determining factor in how you should be eating.

Those who are active are going to require more protein in their diets to make up for the calories burned. Some people need more energy than others, therefore requiring more natural sugars and carbs. You need to pay attention to your individual needs and do what feels best for your own body. The help of a nutritionist or dietician can also be helpful in this case. If you are ever unsure of what you are eating, double-check that it is coming from a natural source and if there are any added ingredients. If you cannot identify what you are eating, then you likely don't need to be eating it.

Anxiety and Depression

Depression is linked to poor gut health.

Mental illness can be very debilitating. Both anxiety and depression will create many problems in your daily life, causing you to feel as though you will never get away from the challenges that you are facing. When your brain is chemically imbalanced, these disorders will form, making you feel sad, worried, and unstable. What was once thought of as a solely mental issue can now be seen in its entirety. Now that you know how the second brain communicates with the main brain, you can really begin to explore the ways in which the gut can impact both anxiety and depression.

Because the flow of dopamine and serotonin must be balanced inside of your body, your gut can cause just as much disruption as your brain. When this type of imbalance occurs, it can be very difficult to prevent and fix. It is not something like a switch that you can just turn on and off. Your habits, genetic predisposition, and general biology will make up for the way that your neurotransmitters operate. With all of the factors involved, you can really see how anxiety and depression can manifest quickly. Of course, outside factors can be a catalyst to mental health difficulties, like losing a loved one, serious illness, or other traumatic life events.

When you begin feeling stressed, your entire body is going to feel these impacts. Because of your fight-or-flight response, your body might decide that it needs to shut down certain systems in order to protect itself. Some examples can include low sexual desire, loss of appetite, and difficulties with digestion. If you have ever felt like your stomach was in knots, it was likely trying to protect you in some way, whether it be from bacteria or a mental challenge that you are experiencing. To your body, this is the only way to ensure that you are protected from the apparent danger.

It is great that your body has this ability, but in turn, this can create an imbalance in your gut microbiome. When your body is trying to protect you, your second brain kicks into action. Since it is no longer simply helping you digest and making sure that things are generally working as they should be, the strength of your gut microbiome can be compromised. This means that more bad bacteria is going to have the opportunity to infiltrate your system.

With this surge in bad bacteria, their activity can cause a corresponding upsurge in the anxiety that you feel. On a normal occasion, the good bacteria will typically help you build up resilience. In an unbalanced body, however, you are going to feel negative impacts. Miguel Toribio-Mateas, Board of Scientific Advisors, goes into detail about the different forms of gut-brain communication that can lead to mental health struggles such as anxiety and depression:

- When you have inflammation inside of your stomach, this can actually contribute to depression, causing a build-up of opportunistic (bad) bacteria. In turn, this will lead to the worsening of the inflammation if the gut bacteria continue to multiply. This proves more than ever that it is important to keep your gut health regular. If you begin to feel an imbalance, you might need to start taking some probiotics to clean out and help regulate your system.
- Research has shown that probiotic bacteria are helpful for alleviating both anxiety and depression. Those who take supplements regularly feel better when they might have not even realized that inflammation was occurring in the first place. You can also eat more foods that are rich in prebiotics, such as fruits, vegetables, grains, and legumes.

- It is recommended to eat a variety of different foods that are cooked in different ways. This will give your body more of a chance to diversify and to allow the gut microbes to positively influence your brain. When they are diverse and stimulated, they will produce more serotonin which is going to greatly help your mood.
- In order to understand the complexity of the gut microbiome, it is important to remember that you can control the way that it operates to an extent. There are two approaches that people normally take. The first is the need to investigate every single ill feeling and make strict dietary changes. The second involves letting the body do what it wants to do naturally. There is a middle ground, though. Eating a science-based diet that includes around 30 plant-based foods each week will help ensure that the gut stays as healthy as possible.

Emotional Health

Even if you have never suffered from anxiety or depression before, paying attention to your emotional health is still a smart move to make. No matter what you are doing or where you are in life, your emotional health is important. It is the voice that is playing in the back of your mind that lets you know if everything is going to be okay or not. You should always do your best to listen to this voice, noticing any changes that might be impacting your daily life. Your emotions can feel fine one day and then they might change the next day — this is normal. As humans, we must endure many different feelings and emotions while trying to sort through all of the information that we are given. This can be overwhelming for some people.

For those who are typically balanced when it comes to their emotional health, all it takes is a single stressor for everything to feel as though it has turned around. What used to be manageable can seem like a task that is never going to end. Know that this is also a normal feeling and that there are things that you can do to ease the worry. The next time that you feel uncertainty regarding your emotional health, one thing that you can start with is an observation of your gut health. Since the two are very closely linked, you might be able to find some clues as to what is going on.

While focusing on your gut health won't necessarily take away your stressors, it will allow your body to have a fighting chance. With a strong enteric nervous system, you won't have to work so hard to produce the necessary serotonin that your brain needs in order to remain mentally balanced. Again, start by taking a look at your eating habits. Not only do you need to pay attention to what you are consuming, but when and how. If you have a habit of eating a lot of processed food right before you sleep, it is natural to assume that your body is having trouble digesting this.

When this occurs, your second brain is working overtime to try and digest the food that you are giving it. When it is more waste than nutrition, it is as though you are overexerting your digestive system. The more junk food that you eat, the more your body is going to be working hard for a minimal result. This is why you should consider eating foods that are more balanced and full of nourishment. While you don't have to give up on your junk food favorites entirely, you should start practicing moderation.

Allow yourself to have treats as a form of reward, but do not make them the main food group in your diet. Your body should be more focused on the vitamins and minerals that it is getting rather than the processed flavors and sugars. After a prolonged period of time, you are not going to be functioning nearly as well as you can. What you put into your body is going to directly impact the way that you feel and what you are able to accomplish, both physically and mentally. Changing your diet goes beyond losing weight and exercising. It changes your internal systems, allowing them to work better for you.

Every time you experience a stomach ache, or a bloated feeling, don't just assume that your body is trying to digest your food and that it will pass on its own. It is your body trying to tell you that it needs help to process what you are providing. Take small steps to see if you notice a difference. Add more fruits and vegetables to your current diet and see if you can feel anything positive. You can also diversify what you are eating by cooking it in different ways and seasoning it with different flavors. Do all that you can for yourself because your gut health is going to help your emotional health tremendously.

Chapter 4: How our Second Brain Influences Diseases and Illnesses

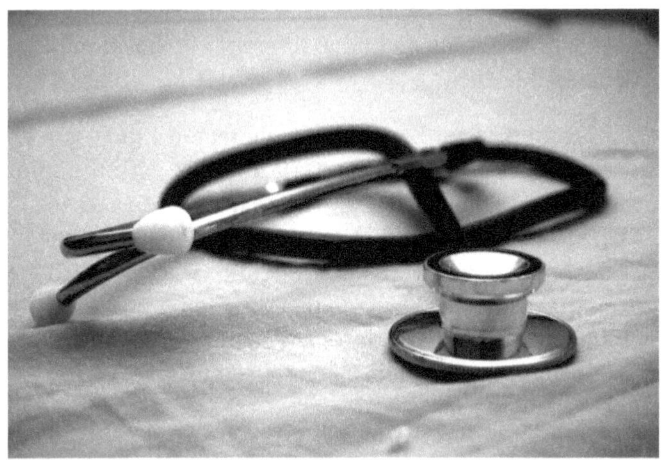

Many illnesses can be avoided when we pay better attention to our overall health.

While you might feel that you are doing everything that you can externally to stay healthy, there are many internal factors that can contribute to many different illnesses. You already know how important it is to keep your gut healthy in order to digest properly and to keep your mood up, but it is also essential to keep it healthy for the purposes of your longevity. Many chronic diseases and illnesses stem from the way that you take care of your second brain. The better you take care of yourself, the healthier you will remain in the future. This chapter takes a look at some common illnesses and showcases just how much your gut can influence them.

Alzheimer's

Alzheimer's is a disease that can progress rapidly over time, killing brain cells as they degenerate. Alzheimer's is the most common cause of dementia, creating a decline in the way that you are able to think and behave. Studies have been done on the impact that gut bacteria have on the progression of Alzheimer's and the findings were surprising — research that came from the University of Lund in Sweden discovered that imbalanced gut bacteria can be linked to the development of the disease. Using mice in their trial, they found that those with Alzheimer's had a different composition of gut bacteria than those who were considered healthy.

For anyone, the composition of gut bacteria is a big factor in how you are going to feel. This occurs because of the way that the bacteria interact with the immune system. If your body feels the need to constantly fight against itself due to an inactive immune system, you are likely to feel sickly and sluggish more often. Another finding from the study done at the University of Lund was that the mice who had Alzheimer's also had a lot more plaque on their brains. This plaque can end up causing lumps that will accelerate the disorder and make it harder for the body to fight off the disease.

Because there is no cure for Alzheimer's, what matters most is how to preserve the brain. To the best of your ability, you need to be aware of how you are treating both of your brains and what you are doing to protect it. Through these findings, it is more apparent than ever that your gut microbiomes need to be balanced in order to avoid developing diseases that can rapidly progress without a cure. Through the research done on the mice, scientists are working on finding new ways to delay or prevent the onset of Alzheimer's and to prevent plaque build-up on the brain.

The research is nowhere near completed because of the complexities of the interactions between the two systems. Through a change of diet and addition of probiotics, scientists are hoping to develop techniques that can change your gut bacteria in an effort to lower the amount of plaque that develops on your brain. Scientists are also hoping that they can discover breakthroughs on how to fully treat the disease rather than only providing minor symptom-relief. They are hoping that more effective treatment methods will come as a result of this research.

Autism

Puzzles are one way to exercise the main brain. Eating well, and controlling stress, keeps the second brain happy and healthy.

John Cryan, a biochemist at University College Cork in Ireland, was one of the first researchers to investigate the potential link between autism and the gut microbiome. One finding was that gut bacteria generate by-products as they help to digest food. These by-products can potentially change the way that you think and behave. Clostridia is one example; these are bacterial pathogens that generate propionic acid in your gut. In a study done on rats, it was observed that propionic acid could cause autism-like symptoms, such as unpredictable motor skills and a pattern of repetition.

When you have a deficit in your good bacteria, this might also cause changes in your social brain function. In 2017, Cryan used mice with autism-like conditions to find that their gut made less tryptophan and bile acid. These are both compounds that are needed in order to produce serotonin. In children who suffer from autism, it is often found that they are missing certain beneficial gut bacteria that can be creating similar results.

Another study has shown that those who are on the autism spectrum might potentially have a very porous blood to brain barrier. This means that toxic bacteria have a better chance of being able to enter the bloodstream. It will also quickly be able to have access to the brain.

At the California Institute of Technology in Pasadena, researchers transferred microbes from those with autism to mice in order to better reveal how this causes developmental issues. At six-weeks-old, offspring of the mice were seen socializing less. They also made less noise and seemed to pick up on more repetitive behavior. In a direct comparison, the mice without these genes present seemed to develop on a normal path and were able to interact well with others.

While this does not necessarily prove that an improperly balanced gut microbiome *causes* autism, there are definitely a few linked behaviors that can form as a result of having an imbalance of certain bacteria in your system. Scientists agree that more research must be done before they can fully agree on how much of a role your gut bacteria plays in the development of autism. They hope to create more studies with larger control groups in the future. Currently, there are still no medications that are approved for the treatment of autism that covers all of the core challenges. These areas include difficulties in communicating, repetitive behavior, and social challenges.

Cardiovascular Health

According to Harvard Medical School, the last 10 years have been rich with research on understanding the connection of your gut health to your heart health. As a result of this research, two big findings were uncovered. The first is that each microbe inside of your stomach actually has over 100 times as many genes as the traditional human gene. All of their genes as a collective is what makes up our microbiome. The second finding is that a lot of the proteins made by the microbiome are comparable to the proteins made by our own genes. Because these proteins are able to travel through the bloodstream, it is plausible that they can carry bacteria straight to the heart.

In the way that your gut bacteria can determine whether or not you might develop type 2 diabetes, it can also influence the level of bad cholesterol that you have in your body. Without enough good bacteria to protect your body, you are likely going to be at-risk for developing heart disease and high blood pressure. Another plausible concern is that bacteria can affect the plaque in your arteries. Most heart attacks occur when this plaque ruptures, causing a blockage. It is very important that you keep your arteries clear so that the blood is able to successfully flow through them. If you have enough bad bacteria in your gut, this can reduce your arteries' ability to widen, while simultaneously creating too much plaque. This is a very dangerous combination, obviously.

Long story short, the bacteria in your gut is definitely something that can put your heart in danger. Scientists are still trying to define exactly how this connection works and how to prevent it from worsening over time. While there are not sufficient treatments that handle gut bacteria in an effort to prevent heart disease, there are preventative measures that you can take to make sure that your heart stays strong and healthy. It all starts by putting a priority on your gut health. When you can see how valuable the connection is, you will feel more motivated to eat right and to keep your gut microbiome happy.

Irritable Bowel Syndrome (IBS)

Irritable bowel syndrome is a commonly experienced illness that can create an uproar in your life. As a whole, the bacteria in your digestive tract, specifically your intestines, is referred to as your gut flora. In an ideal situation, all of the bacteria are able to coexist in harmony. Whenever this is disrupted, however, this can lead to a state that is known as intestinal dysbiosis. As a result of this, you will be left with some difficult gastrointestinal symptoms to deal with. When your gut flora is not acting harmoniously, it can be a result of many different things such as food poisoning, a poor diet, or the side effects of taking certain antibiotics.

Research has surfaced that suggests IBS can develop in some individuals after they experience an acute bacterial infection in the digestive system. It is thought that out of those who suffer from such an infection, about 25% will continue to experience unpleasant symptoms. This can continue to occur up to six months after the infection has healed. What defines IBS is that the symptoms are ongoing. Another study states that one in 10 people who experience an infection like this are likely going to develop IBS as a result of it.

Again, probiotics are seen as a helpful way to lessen the severity of certain symptoms. When given probiotics, those who suffer from IBS have reported that their symptoms have been significantly reduced. Because probiotics are known as the good kind of bacteria, they work to balance out the bad kind that is living in your gut. When this balance is present, the gut flora is able to work together again, rather than against each other.

A controversial new study has emerged that takes a look at the influence of SIBO (small intestinal bacterial overgrowth) and IBS. SIBO is a condition that occurs when there is a lot of "bad" or opportunistic bacteria present in the small intestine. The findings of this new study suggest that SIBO is actually the primary cause of IBS. Researchers have made this point because SIBO is responsible for many of the symptoms that those suffering from IBS deal with, such as bloating, diarrhea/constipation, and hypersensitivity to certain foods.

When testing for SIBO, the amount of hydrogen in the breath is measured. This is done by first measuring the breath and then consuming lactose. A sugar that will not be absorbed by the body, lactose will remain present and will begin to ferment. It is thought that if the hydrogen levels in the breath are high shortly after consuming lactose, SIBO may be present.

This study is controversial because of the question of the accuracy of the breath test. The current conclusion of this study states that the information is relevant for some IBS patients, but not all of them. Still, the research has proven helpful in the way that scientists are now able to further investigate a certain subset of people who are struggling with IBS.

Poor Gut Health

Becoming aware of all the ways that your gut health can impact your overall health, you can see how easily you might develop one of the above illnesses. In general, you should always make sure that you are prioritizing your gut health. If possible, ask your doctor about taking some probiotics to strengthen the number of good bacteria that you have in your stomach. This is going to help ward off the bad bacteria and allow you to build up a tolerance to it. Also, change your eating habits to reflect the gut health that you want. If you continue to eat poorly, your gut is going to act accordingly. As you know, this is not only going to impact your physical health but also your mental health.

Inflammation

Some diseases either lead to chronic inflammation, or are a result of inflammation, which means that your body is always going to be in this state. Some of those diseases include autoimmune disorders, heart disease, and rheumatoid arthritis. You might be wondering what can be done to provide your body with relief.

The best way to combat inflammation is to eat an anti-inflammatory diet. This is going to consist of foods that contain plenty of antioxidants such as berries, apples, artichokes, broccoli, sweet potatoes, and dark leafy greens. The foods that you will want to avoid are dairy products, meat, margarine, and vegetable oil. Without giving up too many of the things you love, you can rebalance your diet in an effort to keep your body from experiencing too much inflammation.

Potential Cures

Though it is too early to say that a healthy gut can cure diseases, or prevent them entirely, we now have a much better understanding of how our gut health, our second brain, interacts with the rest of our body. When the gut is happy, we tend to be less inflamed, so feel less pain and aches, in general. When the gut is happy, that lowered inflammation means our skin looks and feels healthier. When the gut is happy, we experience more mental clarity, and energy/motivation.

Additionally, we see links between inflammation and gut health; inflammation is often a precursor to cancer, heart disease, type 2 diabetes, and a myriad of auto-immune diseases.

Can a healthy gut cure these things? The short answer is, "no." However, it can diminish symptoms, reduce the risk of developing chronic illnesses, and bring about a general feeling of health and wellness.

Chapter 5: How our Second Brain Improves our First Brain

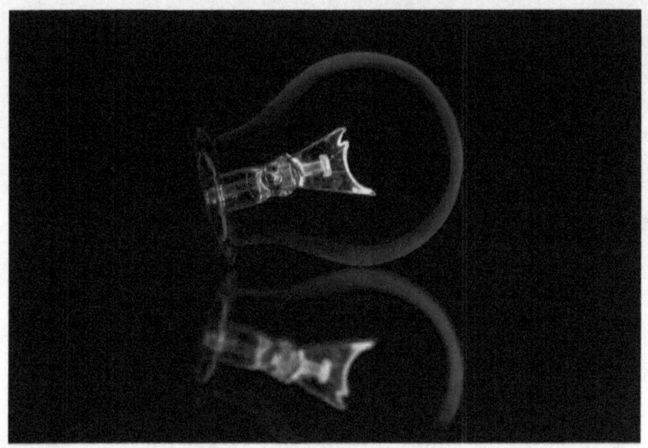

What's the connection between our first and second brain?

After realizing how much power the second brain has, it is natural to think about the ways in which it can end up improving the first brain. With a fully functional system like, you can experience improvements in your memory, cognitive ability, athletic ability, and productivity. Overall, nearly every area of your brain health has something to do with your gut health. In this chapter, you will see exactly how your second brain allows your first brain to become stronger.

Memory

When considering how the second brain impacts your memory, you must have an understanding of the role that glutamate plays. It is the most abundant neurotransmitter that is found in your brain and your central nervous system. In nearly every major excitatory brain function that you have, you can be certain that glutamate is going to be involved. To define "excitatory," you can think of the neurotransmitter as an action that increases the likelihood that a neuron will fire based on its influence. This is considered an action potential. When this occurs, it can be compared to what happens to an electrical circuit that powers a light switch. Glutamate is a crucial neurotransmitter because it is the main component when it comes to neural circuit communication.

Glutamate and GABA (gamma-aminobutyric acid) are connected. While you know that glutamate is an excitatory neurotransmitter, GABA is the complete opposite. It is best known for being the most prominent inhibitor in the central nervous system. GABA decreases the likelihood that a neuron will fire. When you understand how these neurotransmitters are working together in your body, you will find that an imbalance of one can make a big difference in the way that you think and feel.

Groups of neurons form circuits in your brain that carry out small-scale functions. This can come in the form of recalling a memory that you have or creating a new memory. When inner-connected, these circuits can create large-scale networks that are responsible for more complex functions such as your vision and your hearing. It is important that all of these cells work together as one in order to allow you to be a fully functional version of yourself. This becomes possible with consistent communication between the cells.

Think of your neurotransmitters as the chemical messenger system in your brain. The way that these neurotransmitters work has everything to do with the way you are going to function. Just like any miscommunication, this can lead to some consequences. If you want to ensure that your body and mind know what to do, you need to have a healthy internal communication system. Glutamate plays a large role because it is involved with synaptic plasticity; the ability for a neuron's signal to strengthen or weaken over time. This does a lot to shape your memory and to dictate your ability to learn new things.

To better understand how glutamate signaling works, there is a principle that has been developed based on the Goldilocks fable. It is sometimes referred to as the Goldilocks Principle. In the tale, Goldilocks tastes the three bears' bowls of porridge. One is too cold, one is too hot, and the last one is just right. Your level of glutamate also needs to be just right because having too much or too little can result in issues with your memory. This principle has become a common concept in cognitive science, easily illustrating how "more" isn't always better. There is such a thing as "too much of a good thing."

Glutamate is a prime example of the Goldilocks Principle because too much can damage your nerve cells while too little will cause you to have difficulty concentrating and other mental exhaustion. Scientists remind us that we need to avoid black-and-white thinking when considering the roles that glutamate plays because nothing in the body has one simple answer. The only focus should be on getting just the right amount of glutamate in your system in an effort to balance out your brain. This can be said for your other neurotransmitters, as well.

One of the easiest ways to obtain more glutamate is by eating certain foods. Luckily, you will be able to find it in any food that contains protein. Since glutamate is an amino acid, you can think of it as a building block of protein. Some foods that naturally contain glutamate are cheese, milk, meat, fish, and mushrooms. These are likely foods that you already consume on a regular basis, which becomes a great sign for ensuring that you are getting enough glutamate in your system.

It is important that you understand the difference between glutamate and MSG (monosodium glutamate). MSG is the salty part of glutamate and it is usually used to flavor foods. The makeup of MSG is simple, only containing water, sodium, and glutamate. It is not as nutritionally beneficial as glutamate because it is only meant to enhance flavors that are already found in foods instead of assisting your brain's memory function. Having this awareness of the presence of MSG is important because your body won't be able to treat it any differently than it treats glutamate. Therefore, you might experience headaches, nausea, chest pain, and other negative side effects after you consume it.

Cognitive Function

Can our thinking improve when our gut microbiome is healthy?

Your cognitive function refers to your ability to handle many different mental functions. This includes your ability to learn, think, remember, reason, make decisions, and solve problems. These are all basic skills that you need in order to live your life every single day. All of your brain chemistry works together to influence your cognitive function.

Putting all of the pieces together, you can probably see how your second brain plays a role because of the way that it communicates with your main brain.

Supported by specific neuron networks, these systems must have excellent communication in order to tell your brain what must be done. As you get older, these skills tend to naturally decline. Any time that you aren't using functions on a regular basis, it will become harder for your brain to recall and perform them. The good news is that you can look for ways to boost your cognitive functions in your efforts to take better care of yourself and your gut health.

Using the following example, you will see just how connected your second brain and first brain become when a cognitive function must be used:

Imagine that you are having a rough start to your morning. Even though you woke up on time, everything seems to be going wrong and you are getting stressed out. Because you cannot find the work presentation that you must bring with you, the time that you would have spent eating breakfast has instead been devoted to searching for this project. With only a few minutes remaining before you must leave the house, you find the project and then you must rush out the door on an empty stomach.

Think about what this might do to the rest of your day, and you can likely come to the conclusion that you are going to feel stressed, maybe even jittery. Since you didn't eat and you are stressed out, your body is going to crave comfort foods that are high in carbs, fats, or sugars in an effort to make your brain feel better - at least for the short-term.

These cravings come about because your second brain sends signals to your main brain, insisting that your stomach needs these foods in order to allow you to function properly. Stress-management is highly essential when you are trying to balance out your mind and body. If you allow stress to take over your life, you are only going to be giving in to your second brain's emergency response as an effort to make you feel better. While you might feel better at the moment, you know that eating junk food and being stressed out without any true resolution is not the best way to take care of yourself. As a result of this, you are also relying less on your cognitive functions and more on your coping mechanisms.

Create a plan for yourself when you begin to feel stressed or overwhelmed. Know that you are going to have options for what to do in case you feel that you are in over your head. When you give in to these feelings, you are telling your main brain that it can give in. Instead of using the skills and abilities that you know you have, it can be easier to just give in when something feels too hard. You need to exercise your cognitive abilities if you want them to continue serving you in the future. Ignoring them will only trigger other reactions from your body and your second brain. You might unintentionally develop bad habits that will need to be corrected.

Get into the habit of listening to what your body is telling you before you jump straight into a defense mechanism, or a stress response. When you feel that you are mentally overwhelmed and your second brain is encouraging you to eat, consider that you might not actually be hungry at that moment. If you do feel that you could benefit from eating something, try your best to consume foods that are rich in brain-healthy nutrients that will encourage your brain to function well instead of placing it into a sluggish state after consuming copious amounts of sugar and junk food.

Athletic Function and Productivity

When your second brain is functioning properly, this is going to directly influence your athletic function as well as your productivity. It is no secret that exercising and being active helps you feel great. You don't have to work out multiple times a day to feel the benefits of the endorphins as they rush through your system. Much like other functions, you are going to become better at physical activity the more that you do it. By exercising your muscles, they become stronger and your endurance allows you to go for longer. Overall, being active creates many positive chain reactions that can allow you to live a very beneficial lifestyle.

Have you ever tried to go for a run after eating a heavy meal? Chances are you either had a stomach ache or could not perform to the best of your ability, perhaps both. Thinking about your second brain and the way that physical activity depends on its health will allow you to have yet another reason to stay healthy. Common sense is all that it takes to ensure that you are doing what is best for your body. If you know that you need exercise to stay healthy, you should be able to pick the best times to do this physical activity. You should be able to make time for anything that is important to you, so don't allow time to become your excuse.

Eating the foods that are going to boost your metabolism will help keep your second brain healthy and active. Try to incorporate plenty of these ingredients in your diet:

- Spinach
- Avocados
- Beans
- Apples
- Celery

- Almonds
- Grapefruit
- Garlic
- Whole Grains (in moderation)
- Lentils
- Green Tea
- Water
- Coffee (in moderation)

When your body knows how to burn fat and create muscle, you are going to notice great physical benefits when you get active. Your athletic function will be on the rise, as long as you are willing to train and work in a self-disciplined manner. Exercise because it makes you feel good, not because you feel forced to. When you actually enjoy what you are doing, it is going to be a lot more fun to stay active and to pay attention to your gut health.

In terms of productivity, you know that it requires a lot of brainpower to stay focused. When you aren't able to concentrate, you are going to find yourself unable to complete tasks or you'll make mistakes that you would not have normally made. Just like any other muscle in your body, you need to make sure that you exercise your brain, as well. You can do this by completing activities known as brain-teasers to keep yourself thinking quickly and efficiently. Doing brain exercises on a regular basis will ensure that you aren't becoming lazy. When you only focus on the same things over and over again, this does not give your brain the chance to think outside of the box. Make sure that you are regularly processing new information and learning how to explore ideas creatively to encourage yourself to think differently.

Your gut health is directly connected to your brain health because it can impact the way that communication is happening. While you know that the second brain communicates to the main brain frequently, you need to have adequate nutrients in your system if you want your second brain to create the necessary neurotransmitters that will become beneficial to your brain. As discussed, when taking a look at how anxiety and depression can develop, your second brain needs to be healthy in order to generate all of the right chemistry in your main brain.

When you have an adequate amount of those feel-good chemicals in your brain, it is going to be a lot easier to stay motivated and productive. You are going to feel that you are able to complete the goals that you set for yourself and that you are making progress each day. Part of staying on top of your productivity comes from always giving yourself something to work toward. From there, you need to keep yourself motivated to complete these things.

Chapter 6: The Importance of Your Diet for Your Gut Health

Food for a happy gut microbiome includes fresh, whole vegetables and fruit.

We've touched on this throughout the preceding chapters - you are what you eat.

This is more than just a saying. The food that you consume breaks down and directly becomes a part of your functioning systems. Through a filtering process, your second brain gets to decide which parts to keep and which parts to turn into waste. By having better control of what you are putting into your body, you are going to experience the positive benefits that come from eating well that can include more energy, better brain function, and a faster metabolism. Overall, the diet that you have is the most important way that you can ensure the health of your second brain.

Wholesome Food and Its Benefits

When you hear that someone consumes a "whole food" diet, you might be wondering what exactly qualifies as whole food. In nutritional terms, eating this way means that you are eating food that is unaltered by preservatives or artificial flavors. The food is eaten the way that it is grown and it is only seasoned with natural herbs and spices.

Some people also refer to this as eating "clean." No matter how you address it, eating wholesome food is going to make a big difference in your overall health. When you can rid your body of the artificial toxins that are found in other foods, you are going to feel a lot happier and a lot more energized.

Eating wholesome foods means that you are consuming necessary nutrients that aid with your various bodily functions. This means that the foods are actually going to be helpful with processing this nourishment and turning it into energy or muscle. They will also require less filtering which means that it will result in less waste and fat production. When you eat foods that are nutritionally beneficial, your body is going to have much more of a use for them than it would with junk food.

But, let's be honest. There is some satisfaction that comes from eating junk foods or comfort foods, but after digestion, your body is only going to either turn it into waste or add it to your fat storage. In the end, your body will have worked very hard to actually ingest food that isn't going to provide you with any nutrients. Therefore, you might end up feeling sluggish or even depressed as a result of this. Proper nutrients are required if you want to have a diet that supports your physical health as well as your mental health.

Since wholesome foods also contain plenty of fiber, that will aid in your digestion and speed up your metabolism. As you know, your gut health is dependent on these two factors. The more fiber that you consume, the more full that you will feel. There is no worse feeling than eating to only crave more food because you are still unsatisfied. When you can find foods to eat that are rich in fiber, that feeling of fullness will not only come sooner, but it will also last longer. You'll also find that your general digestive health improves.

Different Food for Different Life Stages

Dietary needs change as we grow older.

Childhood

As a child, you need the highest number of macronutrients and micronutrients during any developmental stage of life. This is because you are going to do the most growing, both physically and mentally, during this time. Because children grow so rapidly, they need a lot more energy in order to keep up with their growth. It is thought that the average child needs around 83 calories per kilogram on a daily basis, as compared to the 30 that adults usually need.

Protein is also very important for children to support all of the growth that will be taking place. Keep in mind that bone density should also be something that is focused on because children need to have strong and healthy bones while they are going through all of these growth spurts. Dairy can help increase their bone density and provide them with a strong foundation for their later years. Making sure that children also drink plenty of water will keep them feeling hydrated and prevent any bathroom-related difficulties that can develop as they expand their palettes.

Healthy foods for children include:

- Lean meat like chicken
- Milk
- Cheese
- Eggs
- Whole grain cereals
- Protein-rich nuts and legumes
- A wide variety of vegetables
- Fruit like apples, pears, grapefruit, strawberries

Adulthood

As you age, you need to maintain your physical and mental health to the best of your ability. Most adults will slow down as they age because of certain work situations and a general decline in energy levels. To prevent life from slowing you down, you need to make sure that you are getting enough foods that contain vitamins K, C, B1, B2, and B3. Magnesium and zinc are also recommended. This, paired with an exercise routine, will keep you feeling energized and healthy as an adult.

Healthy foods for adults include:

- Oranges
- Bell peppers
- Leafy greens
- Fish
- Lean meats
- Eggs
- Yogurt
- Legumes
- Nuts and seeds

Later Years

When you reach your later years in life, your body is going to slow down a bit more. This happens both naturally and due to your ability to maintain mobility. The healthier that you eat in your earlier stages of life will set the guideline for how healthy you will eat in your later years. It is important to form these habits early on because they can be difficult to reverse if you are not used to them. You must also keep in mind that you are going to face certain age-related ailments throughout the years that can prevent you from eating as well or as much as you used to. If you have any diseases or disorders that have developed, you are going to need to plan your diet around them. Your digestive tract, for example, might have difficulty digesting the same foods that you used to eat and it can also become incredibly sensitive to foods that have additives included.

There are certain similarities to the way that you ate as an infant to the way that you need to eat as a senior. Bone density is fragile during both of these stages of life, so making sure that you get enough calcium is essential. You will also need to pay close attention to your digestive system. As you age, it can become difficult to process certain foods because your body has less energy to break them down.

Healthy foods for seniors include:

- Apples
- Blueberries

- Oranges
- Carrots
- Sweet potatoes
- Brown rice
- Whole-grain pasta
- Whole-grain crackers
- Dairy products like milk and cheese
- Fish
- Lean meats

Foods to Avoid

When eating a diet that is supposed to promote gut health, you need to be aware of certain foods that will set your progress back. Since you now know how important eating well is for your gut health and your overall health, you can focus on eating well for your health. Being on a diet is not for everyone, but isn't about "dieting." Really, it's more about knowing how to eat properly, and forming new habits that will serve you long into the future.

1. Sugar: When you eat too much sugar, this is going to create problems with your digestive health. Sugar can lead to constipation and poor gut function for those who are consuming a high-sugar diet. Excess sugar consumption, in all its forms (including grains), leads to blood sugar dysregulations, type 2 diabetes, and heart disease. It is always wise to be aware of how much sugar you are consuming, both natural and otherwise.
2. Artificial Sweeteners: You'd think these would be ok for you, but they are, in fact, known to be even worse than natural sugar. Artificial sweeteners have become popular among those who are trying to lose weight. However, they actually create many negative impacts on your gut health, including changing your gut microbial composition and increasing your glucose intolerance. This creates more opportunities for the development of metabolic diseases like type 2 diabetes, high cholesterol levels and obesity.
3. Soy: You might be thinking that you have only heard that soy is a healthy component to your diet, but too much can prove to have adverse effects. As we've mentioned before - there is "too much of a good thing." In limited quantities, soy can be an excellent source of protein and natural estrogens. However, consuming too much soy can create damage to your gut microbiome. For instance, excess soy

consumption has been shown to reduce your "good" Bifidobacteria and Lactobacillus levels.

4. Processed Foods: While a lot of people are aware that processed foods are not good for any diet, their taste still draws people in. Processed food can disturb your gut health so much, however, that they can eventually lead to colitis and metabolic disease. No matter how good it tastes, consider the implications of eating too much processed food in your diet. Moderation is key here.

5. Red Meat: While consuming some is not likely to be very harmful, consuming too much red meat can encourage certain bacterial growth that will actually negatively impact your health. Not only can it lead to weight gain, but it can also impact your emotional state of being. When you consume red meat, choose grass-fed beef as it is higher in healthy Omega-3 fatty acids, and less inflammatory than corn-fed beef.

Again, the key to eating anything from the above list is doing so in moderation. If you do have some of these foods on occasion, they are unlikely to cause any permanent adverse effects. As long as you are aware of your levels of consumption, you should have no problems avoiding the ingredients as you move forward. When you have something from the "avoid" list, counter it with two healthy foods - just make sure that doesn't result in eating too many overall calories. Another option is if you go to a party, for example, and have lots of "junk," eat really well for the next couple of days to give your body a chance to recover and get some good nutritional balance in its system.

There are going to be times when you crave these things and you do not need to punish yourself if you do end up consuming them. Keep in mind that you can always stick to a gut-healthy diet, as long as you are willing to lessen the number of bad foods that you consume. The more that you do this, the better you will begin to feel.

Helpful Diets

If you do wish to follow a specific diet to curb your eating habits, make sure that you select one that promotes gut health. The following diets contain benefits for both your second brain as well as your first. They are varied and nutritious, giving you plenty of options when it comes to the food that you can safely eat. Adhering to a diet that isn't limited is easy and beneficial. It will allow you to feel great physically and also feel at peace mentally.

DASH

The DASH diet stands for Dietary Approaches to Stop Hypertension. It is a diet designed to provide you with a low-fat menu while still allowing you to have plenty of protein. To get your protein, it is recommended that you eat plenty of fish and poultry. You can also eat nuts if you need a little bit extra. Red meats and sugary foods are to be avoided. The DASH diet places a focus on eating enough fiber and calcium, so you can expect to eat many different fruits, vegetables, and whole grains as well. It is a great and well-rounded diet that can eliminate the inflammation that you often develop inside your body.

Research has shown that it works because it is a diet that is focused on your overall health, not just a single area of your health. When you take this kind of approach, you can be sure that you are taking real preventative measures toward the decline of your brain health and your gut health. People both young and old have seen great benefits from being on the DASH diet.

Foods to eat:

- Salmon
- Poultry
- Leafy greens
- Low-fat cheese and milk
- Broccoli
- Bell peppers
- Oranges
- Carrots
- Blueberries
- Nuts and seeds
- Apples
- Whole grains

Mediterranean

The Mediterranean diet, as the name implies, is adapted from the diets of individuals who live in the Mediterranean areas of Spain, Italy, Greece and Northern Africa. This diet has been studied for decades and is well-known to be great at helping you stay healthy and eliminating certain risk factors for disease. It also allows you to stay full without forcing yourself to eat foods that you do not enjoy. The Mediterranean diet is so open that most people who are on it don't even feel like they are on a diet at all. With the flexibility to accommodate most palettes, many people have seen great success while being on this diet. Most people stay on it for life after seeing how beneficial it is.

The diet offers a pyramid model of the foods you should be eating. Fruits, vegetables, nuts, whole grains, and vegetable oils account for the base of the pyramid. Fish is recommended at least twice per week. Poultry and dairy should be consumed moderately and sparingly. Red meats and sugars are to be eaten much less often than the rest of the groups. By following this model, you will be able to supercharge your body and leave yourself feeling great. Not only does it have the potential to make you physically stronger, but it can also strengthen the health of your brain.

Foods to eat:

- Apples
- Carrots
- Blueberries
- Nuts and seeds
- Rice
- Crackers
- Pasta
- Salmon
- Trout
- Tuna
- Poultry
- Cheese and milk

Chapter 7: Fasting for Gut Health

Water consumption is critical for gut health.

While there are many common misconceptions about the idea of fasting and how to fast properly, there are actually many health benefits that go along with the process when you know how to do it effectively. When you fast, it's like pressing the "reset button" on your various systems and bodily functions. It gives you the chance to get better acquainted with the state of your current health and allows you to make any changes in a controlled and easy way.

As you fast, you will not have to think about how hungry you feel or how depleted your energy levels are. Instead, you will be able to find the method that works for you that will allow your body to reset itself while still taking care of your basic needs. The trick to fasting properly is by following a specific method. When you want to fast, you need to do more than simply stop eating. You have to understand the way that your body works and how fasting is going to impact each part. Your gut health will have the chance to be rejuvenated and renewed after you successfully complete your fasting experience.

Improvements

In the last few years, fasting and taking care of your gut health have made medical breakthroughs. It is now proven that combining the two can create even more positive results for you. Not only will your gut health be at its prime, but you will also feel happier and fitter. Because fasting can help protect your gut microbiome, the bacteria can then turn around and protect you while you are fasting. Acting together as one unit, you are going to be able to see an endless chain of great results. There is also evidence that has been widely discussed about fasting being helpful for your immune system. As you know, your immune system needs to remain strong if you are going to be able to fight against any bad bacteria in your body.

Brand new research has shown that fasting can actually activate your anti-inflammatory response. This means that it will protect you from getting sick and it will also continue to protect your good gut bacteria that serve its purpose. Overall, the positive outcomes of fasting seem to point to great results. It is important to understand that fasting is only a single component of your healthcare regime that you should not overestimate. When done correctly and combined with a proper diet and exercise routine, you will be able to feel its full benefits for yourself. Know that this is just one additional step that can be taken on the journey to a healthier second brain.

The idea behind fasting is very simple, no matter which method you choose. Its principle is basic — abstain from eating food for a given period of time. By doing so, your body will be able to process through each of its critical functions without having to work as hard because it isn't trying to digest food simultaneously. You can think about fasting as letting your body run a cleaning cycle. If there is any bacteria or harmful germs lingering, fasting will allow your body to find it all and make an attempt to get rid of it.

Aside from allowing you to cleanse yourself, fasting can also help you lose weight. Making sure that you are not overweight goes hand-in-hand with managing your gut health. If you are carrying a lot of excess weight, your body isn't going to function as well as it can. Know that losing weight does not have to involve any extreme measures. Many people believe that fasting is extreme, but that is because they do not understand how it works. When you control what you eat in this way and allow your body to catch up, it is going to work more efficiently.

Fasting does not mean that you must go for days without food, starving yourself. When you fast to lose weight, you are going to be experiencing periods of consuming food followed by the fasting periods. You should not feel that you are being deprived of anything or that you are suffering. If you feel this way, you are doing something wrong.

Peter LePort, M.D. is the medical director of the MemorialCare Center for Obesity at Orange Coast Memorial Medical Center. He advises that fasting is safe for most people to try. Of course, it is best to get a medical opinion from your own doctor before you attempt to incorporate fasting into your gut health regimen. Understand that you need to do it properly or else you are going to end up experiencing adverse effects.

Different Types of Fasting

As mentioned, there are many ways that you can fast. The following are two of the most common options used by individuals who want to take better care of their gut and overall health. By understanding their differences, you should be able to make an informed decision of which option is going to work best for you and for your lifestyle.

Intermittent Fasting

This form of fasting is also known as time-restricted feeding. It is the process of only eating food during specific times each day in an effort to control your intake. The two windows are known as the "feeding" and "fasting" windows. Both are fairly self-explanatory. You are to eat during the feeding windows and fast during the other. When you are in a period of fasting, you aren't supposed to consume anything with calories. This means that water and other no-calorie beverages (but still avoid artificial sweeteners) are okay to consume. This prevents you from becoming dehydrated and sick. This period of time also allows you to drink black coffee and herbal teas. Some experts even recommend that you can drink no-calorie sports beverages that boost your electrolytes. As long as you make sure that you are staying away from sports drinks that are high in sugar, or have artificial sweeteners, you should be able to consume them.

When you fast this way, your body experiences a productive eating pattern that can promote weight loss. Even if that is not your aim, intermittent fasting can still improve your body's fat-burning ability, improve your insulin sensitivity, improve your heart health, and lower your blood sugar levels. With all of these benefits, it seems crazy that intermittent fasting can also make a positive influence on your gut health. It works by giving your gut a break. When you are constantly eating, or eating sporadically, your body is always in work mode. Intermittent fasting creates boundaries for your body.

Intermittent fasting allows you to have an empty digestive tract for part of the time, telling your body that it is okay to rest. This is why many people who fast this way report feeling even more energized than before. Intermittent fasting also encourages your gut to adhere to its circadian rhythm. Your gut microbes will perform better this way and your body will have a better understanding of when it is supposed to enter its metabolic state.

There are three simple ways you can try intermittent fasting for yourself:

1. The 16:8 Protocol: Eat food during an eight-hour window and fast for the remaining 16 hours. This is a good method for those who are just starting out with fasting because your time spent sleeping will make up for half of these hours that you will be fasting.
2. The Warrior Diet: For this method, you are supposed to fast for 20 hours and eat during a four-hour window. This method works best for those who have some prior fasting experience, as the fast is going to last longer than the previous method. It is not recommended for those who struggle with binge-eating disorders or other preexisting conditions.
3. Alternate-Day Fasting: As it sounds, this method teaches you to eat normally one day and then restrict your eating the next day. On your fasting days, you are supposed to consume around 500-600 calories.

Water Fast

The next method of fasting to be discussed is water fasting. This process is simple because it only involves two basic steps — eating to prepare for the fast, and then drinking only water during the fast. On average, you should be drinking around 10 glasses of water each day. This is important to remember if you decide to do a water fast. You need to make sure that you do not get dehydrated, as this can be a difficult method of fasting for beginners at first. You need to aim for three days of water fasting, only consuming your recommended amount of water each day. There is also a preparation process that you should adhere to before you begin.

Limit the amount of meat that you are eating before you start and make sure that you are eating a moderate amount of dairy. This will allow your body to ease into the transition of only surviving off of water. As you make this transition, attempt to eat 75% raw or steamed vegetables and the other 25% healthy, lean proteins. This is going to prepare your body to function well during your fasting experience.

Doing this fast will allow you to experience several health benefits, as seen below:

- Boost in metabolism
- Supports fat loss
- Improves cell recycling (autophagy)
- Protects your brain
- Decreases inflammation
- Promotes a healthy stress response
- Improves cardiovascular health
- Initiates short-term ketosis

When taking a look at all of the benefits of water fasting, you can see why this can potentially be a great step toward taking better care of your gut health. After you have successfully fasted for as long as you want, take care to break the fast properly. Since your body is not used to digesting food anymore, you need to be easy on it. Re-enter your normal routine by slowly introducing food back into the diet. If you feast right away, your stomach is going to have a hard time adjusting. Start with simple, whole foods and work your way back up to eating meals again. Your body will be completely renewed and rejuvenated.

It is generally recommended that you fast for no more than 48-hours - additionally, consult with your physician to ensure that this more extreme fast is safe for you.

Treatment of Diseases

Health matters - eating well, exercising, and controlling stress is great for your brain and heart health.

The benefits of fasting are fascinating because they allow your body to regain its own natural rhythm. Instead of trying to force yourself into eating a particular diet or adhering to an intense workout routine, you can simply allow your body to get back to where it feels it should be on its own. When you enter periods of fasting, you are telling your body that you want it to take back control over your internal systems. The more that your body is able to practice this, the stronger it will become. After reading about the benefits of fasting, you can see why it is great for helping you fight against various diseases and illnesses.

When your heart and brain are healthier, you are giving yourself a brand new way to protect your body against diseases. Because heart and brain illnesses are so common, keeping these two key components of your body healthy will improve your overall well-being. Knowing that they are both going to remain strong will allow you to have some peace of mind, therefore getting rid of a lot of the stress that surrounds staying healthy. Because fasting is so easy, you do not have to worry about doing anything wrong or doing anything potentially harmful to your heart and brain. As long as you follow the steps carefully, you can make sure that you are correctly fasting and allowing your body to get back to the rhythm that it needs to be in.

Since your cells are going to be recycled more frequently during periods of fasting, you can count on your body to create more good cells that are going to protect you. When you get stuck in the same eating habits, especially if they are poor, you aren't giving your body the chance to generate better cells. This is why it can be very easy to get stuck in your bad eating habits, constantly feeling like you are going to get sick and unable to heal quickly when you do get sick.

Inflammation reduction is another very important factor in keeping your body healthy. In any illness or disease, inflammation plays a big role because it can worsen symptoms. The inflammation that develops inside your body puts more stress on your organs, causing them to fight harder to keep you safe. By reducing this inflammation, you can conserve this energy that you would have had to use and put it toward other actions that can further protect you. You will also feel great physical benefits, such as additional mobility and increased endurance. Overall, your body is going to be better able to handle anything that you experience when it is less inflamed.

Chapter 8: Prebiotics and Probiotics

Fruits and vegetables are rich in prebiotics.

You have likely heard the mention of both prebiotics and probiotics when it comes to maintaining your gut health. Many people are often under the misconception that these both have to be medically prescribed, but they are actually accessible to all. With the use of both prebiotics and probiotics, you can give your gut a necessary boost in health so that it will function better and feel better, too. This chapter is going to teach you about all of the different varieties of these products and how they can actually help you. In learning about their protective elements, you are going to wonder why you didn't start taking them even sooner.

Importance on Gut Health

To understand why prebiotics and probiotics are good for your gut, it is important to recognize the benefits that each provides. While they sound similar in name, they offer different health benefits to your second brain. They can even offer benefits to your first brain. Many people take prebiotics and probiotics to supplement certain vitamins and nutrients that the digestive system needs in order to operate smoothly.

Prebiotics

Prebiotic fibers come from the parts of foods that are non-digestible. This fiber travels through your small intestine and becomes fermented by the time it reaches your colon. Some examples of foods that contain prebiotics naturally are bananas, onions, garlic, apple skin, and beans. Though the idea of fermentation sounds like it would give you a stomach ache, this process actually provides you with many different beneficial bacteria strains that you need. It increases the number of good bacteria that you have in your gut. With this increase in good bacteria, you are at less of a risk of developing diseases and your digestive system works better.

Not as fragile as probiotics, prebiotics are not impacted by temperature, time, or stomach acid. The fermentation process is always consistent, despite the individual taking the prebiotics. This makes fiber a reliable resource to use in order to take better care of your gut health. When you take prebiotic fiber on a regular basis, the good bacteria that it promotes can also allow you to have better bone density, regularity with your bathroom usage, weight management, and stronger brain health. Along with supplementing prebiotics, you can incorporate more ingredients that will allow you to make sure that you are getting enough on a regular basis.

Foods to Eat

- Wheat bread: 1 gram of fiber per slice; 70% of total fiber is prebiotic
- Asparagus: 2-3 grams of prebiotic fiber per ½ cup
- Oatmeal: 2 grams of fiber per ½ cup; very high in prebiotic fiber
- Dandelion greens: 4 grams of fiber per ½ cup; mostly prebiotic fiber
- Apple with skin: 2 grams of fiber per ½ apple; 50% prebiotic fiber
- Onions and garlic: 2 grams of fiber per ½ cup; 17% prebiotic fiber

These ingredients are not hard to incorporate into your meals and you likely already consume some of them on a regular basis. By eating more of these foods regularly, you can easily increase the amount of prebiotic fiber that you are consuming before you even begin taking a supplement. When you can do your part to take care of your gut health in a way that is proactive like this, you will experience the benefits right away. Your body requires this fiber to operate and a lack in prebiotics can account for many different health issues that you have likely experienced, such as constipation and bloating.

Probiotics

Probiotics are live bacteria that you can consume. They are created through the natural fermentation process of certain foods such as yogurt and kimchi. Those who take probiotics have reported a decrease in gastrointestinal discomfort. If you frequently experience indigestion and bloating, this means that your digestive system could likely use the help of probiotics to function correctly. Another common way to get probiotics is by drinking kefir, a milk drink that has been fermented to create probiotic cultures. This is a very good way to obtain probiotics because it also simultaneously diversifies the bacteria in your gut.

Kefir actually contains over 50 different types of bacteria, all proving to be beneficial for your gut health. With the consistency of yogurt, you likely won't even realize that kefir is a probiotic. All the bacteria travel through your digestive tract in order to make their way to your colon where they will then settle and break down. There are many different bacteria that hold the title of probiotics, but most commonly, they come from one of the two groups:

Lactobacillus: This is the most common probiotic found in yogurt and other foods that have gone through the fermentation process. Best known for helping people digest lactose, it also helps to improve gut health for avoiding diarrhea.

Bifidobacterium: This is also found in dairy products and it has been known to ease IBS symptoms. While it is naturally found in your large intestine, supplementing this bacteria can help to fight off other harmful bacteria in your body. While preventing constipation and keeping you regular, it also helps to strengthen your immune system. Evidence has also stated that it can even help to reduce carcinogenic enzymes, a great function.

How They Work

Many people wonder how well supplements work and why that human body cannot just create its own prebiotics and probiotics. While the body naturally has a head start with creating some of this on its own, it typically isn't enough to see a real difference in the way that your body functions. Eating foods that contain the two bacteria will only provide you with a little bit of an increase, as well. To see real results that will make a big difference, you need to get a concentrated amount of the bacteria into your system and taking prebiotics and probiotics makes this process a lot easier. You might be able to adjust your diet to consume more foods that have gone through the fermentation process, but taking a supplement is always going to be faster and easier.

Having a strong dietary foundation is necessary, though. As discussed, your diet is going to lay out the groundwork for your overall gut health to begin with. When you can consume plenty of fruits, vegetables, and whole grains, you are already allowing your digestive system to have many vitamins and nutrients that it needs in order to function correctly. You can think about taking prebiotics and probiotics as giving yourself a necessary boost. They help quickly and effectively in a way that would cause you to change your diet a lot more if you were only relying on foods for these bacteria.

It also becomes hard to get all of your good bacteria from your diet because of the kind of food that is consumed in this modern world. Even if you do your best to stay away from these things, you are likely going to be eating food that contains preservatives and additives because these things are very commonly used. Foods that are high in sugar can also threaten your gut health, as you already know. There are many ways in which you can accidentally consume too much and this will impact your gut health significantly. Taking prebiotic and probiotic supplements, along with a sensible diet (as we've covered), will help kickstart your gut health.

Research done by the Scientific Association for Probiotics and Prebiotics has shown that the best amount of fiber to consume on a daily basis is 25g-38g of dietary fiber and 5g-20g of prebiotic fiber. In order to meet these suggestions, it has been found that the most success is seen when consuming the fiber from two sources. These sources are chicory root and oligofructose-enriched inulin (OEI). There is a supplement that is known as Prebiotin Prebiotic Fiber that incorporates both sources in an effort to work flawlessly in your system. It is a full-spectrum fiber that has been shown to nourish bacteria on both sides of your colon.

An important thing to remember about probiotics is that they are only going to benefit you if they are alive. Since they are living cultures, this is going to matter a great deal. These are the cultures that are more sensitive to temperature, time, and your own body. If you are relying on foods to get probiotics, you can see how easily they can be killed off just by the way that the food is prepared and cooked. You likely won't even know if this has occurred because you cannot actually see the cultures with the naked eye. This is why taking probiotics has proven to be so beneficial. Any probiotic drinks or supplements should have a guarantee that the cultures are still living. You will be able to have the peace of mind that you are actually ingesting them and are able to use them to balance your gut microbiome.

Doctors recommend that an individual take both prebiotics and probiotics regularly. The great part about starting your own regimen is that your body should already be used to having both in its system. Although you are going to be increasing the amount, this should not leave you with any negative side effects like you might think it would. Your body is going to take action immediately, absorbing the benefits from both the fiber and the live cultures. It is going to know exactly how to use them and how to protect you from harmful bacteria that enter your system.

Different Forms

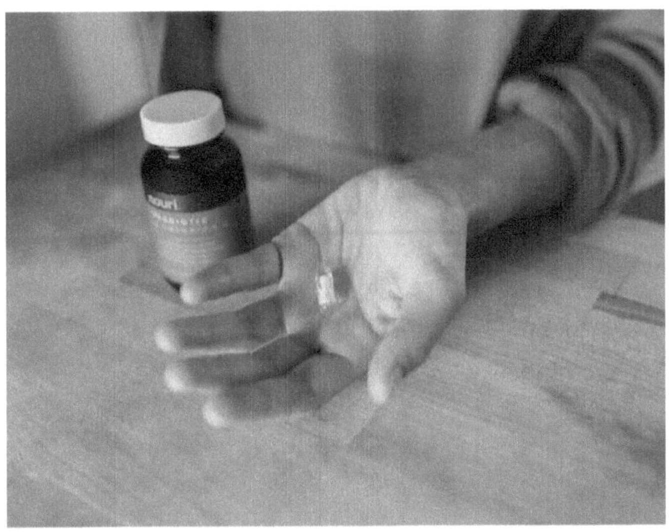

Prebiotics and probiotics come in a variety of forms.

A common way to take prebiotics is through powder form. You should be able to purchase prebiotics at any health store that you shop at. It is simple to take them because you just need to add them to foods that you already eat. Many people enjoy stirring the powder into their oatmeal or adding it into their morning juice. Because it is tasteless, you should not even notice a difference when you begin using the powder. Taking it in the morning is an easy way to boost the good bacteria in your gut and it can become habitual because you should be eating breakfast regularly. It is recommended that you choose a supplement that is of high quality because choosing a lesser one won't provide you with all of the gut health benefits that you are looking for.

If you begin to experience gas while taking your prebiotics, you should pay attention to your dosage. Gastrointestinal problems are your body's way of showing you that you might be consuming too much fiber. Luckily, it should be fairly easy to balance this problem out and consume the right amount for your own body. If you are not comfortable with taking your prebiotics in powder form, you can also take it in pill form. These capsules can be taken just like a vitamin each day, providing you with the right amount of prebiotics very easily. No matter which way you take them, you should be able to notice the benefits right away, as the fiber is going to quickly work its way through your system.

If you want to begin taking probiotics, you can also consume them in a pill form like you can prebiotics. Because these are live cultures that you are dealing with, when you consume them is going to matter. When taking a probiotics pill, it is recommended that you drink a full glass of water with them in order to dilute it so that you can better handle them. Also note, you should take your probiotics shortly before you eat food so that the food can help the cultures work their way into your system gradually. Taking probiotics on an empty stomach might lead to mild side effects such as stomach pain.

When you have an empty stomach, you have an acidic one. This occurs because your pH levels are lower when you are in a fasting state. After taking your probiotics, eating food creates a type of buffering system that will allow the bacteria to travel through your body and eventually reach your large intestine where they need to be. Do your best to create a routine for yourself, much like you would when taking a regular daily vitamin. Life can get busy and it can be easy to forget when to take them, but remember the benefits of taking them in the morning versus waiting too long to take them sporadically throughout the day. You should aim to take them daily and regularly if you want to experience all of their health benefits.

Of course, when attempting to get your daily amount of probiotics, you can always consume kefir. It is like a hybrid between eating food and taking supplements because it is available in a drink form. Some kinds of kefir even come in different flavors, providing you with an enjoyable experience that won't even feel as though you are consuming probiotics. The way that you take your prebiotics and probiotics is up to you and their forms do not make them any more or less effective. The most important thing to remember is that you take them regularly and preferably in the morning. You can take both at the same time, giving your body an overall boost in gut health with benefits that even travel to your main brain. As your body gets used to taking supplements, you might notice slight changes, but these should not be enough to cause you any pain or discomfort. If necessary, you can readjust the dosage of your prebiotics and probiotics that you are taking.

Chapter 9: Psychobiotics

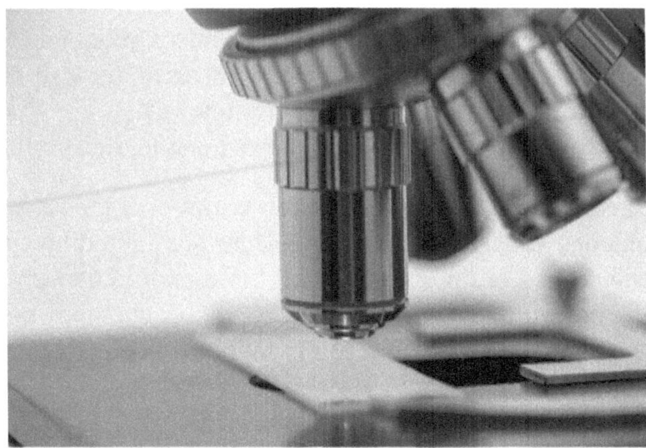

Science is helping us understand how gut health is related to psychological health.

On the same topic of gut health comes another family of helpful bacteria known as psychobiotics. They are lesser known than prebiotics and probiotics, but they offer equally great benefits to your gut health and overall health. When taken on a regular basis, they can even improve mental wellbeing, as well as increasing or balancing serotonin levels.

In this chapter, we'll talk about how psychobiotics work comprehensively in your body. Through new research, we'll explore how the various uses of psychobiotics work to improve mental health, and how scientists foresee their use in the future.

What Are They?

We know that the prefix 'psych' refers to the brain, or mind processes. This form has Greek origins, and literally means, "that which breathes." So, when we talk about psychological processes, we're talking about the human soul, and the breath of life, when we look at it in context to the Greek origins of the word.

Biotic is anything that relates to living things - so, in this realm of getting to know your second brain, psychobiotics might be seen as a way to breathe life into your mental and emotional health.

The practice of using psychobiotics is relatively new, and based on preliminary studies that show the ingestion of live, microscopic organisms, can provide some benefit to those who are struggling with a variety of mental health issues. They are classified as a form of probiotics due to their living nature and the way that they also impact the main brain. During preclinical evaluations done in labs, some psychobiotics actually contain antidepressant and anti-anxiety qualities. This is an extraordinary finding, especially because probiotics are natural and easy to consume. They are known to work by traveling through the vagus nerve, spinal cord, or neuroendocrine system.

As the knowledge about the gut-brain connection grows, it is interesting to observe the ways that psychobiotics can come into play. They are incredibly powerful because having access to the second brain and the main brain simultaneously means that they are going to be helping your body through many processes via many systems. They have the potential to truly change the way that you function for the better, in a way that most medicines cannot even accomplish yet. Because they have only been established since 2013, there is still much more to be discovered about them.

Now that you are familiar with the way that your gut health can directly impact your mental health, consider the amount of stress that you must deal with on a daily basis. If your microbiome is dysfunctional in any way, this is going to cause you to feel the stress more intensely, sometimes, even leading you to feelings of anxiety. By diversifying your microbiome, this problem can possibly be avoided. This is what psychobiotics aim to accomplish. Because they are already diverse enough to heal multiple parts of your body at once, they are known for being great at diversifying your microbiome in an effort to stabilize your mood. When you take them, you should feel as though you are grounded and level, not overwhelmed by the stressors that you regularly encounter. When you can be calm in this way, you know how this can settle your stomach and ease your digestive system, too.

The longer you allow stress to build up and impact you, the more adverse effects you will end up seeing. Stress can begin in one of two areas of your body, either mentally in your brain or physically in your muscles. You have likely experienced both, either feeling as though you cannot slow down the negative thoughts in your mind or feeling as though your muscles are sore and tight because of the tension you are holding onto. No matter which way your stress begins, it is likely to evolve into both physical and mental symptoms because it travels very quickly when left untreated.

Getting stuck at a low point isn't good for you, as you likely already know from personal experience. The more that you ignore stress and difficult things in your life, the more likely you are to develop issues from it in the future. With the help of healthy coping mechanisms, a balanced diet, and psychobiotics, you will find an overall improvement in the way that you are able to live your life. Your mind will be clear and ready to take on what lies ahead and your body will feel relaxed and fully functional in the process. This is an ideal state of being that psychobiotics aims to help you achieve.

How Do You Use Psychobiotics?

After you have done your research on psychobiotics, you can take the next step by consuming them regularly. You can do this in many different ways, just like you can with any other live cultures. To start, make sure that you are taking a low dose. As you get used to them, you can build up your dose, but it makes sense to start on the smaller scale when you are first beginning to take them. This gives your body the chance to adjust to them properly without overwhelming your system. Just like standard probiotics, you might notice some slight side effects if you take too much at once. You may want to work with a health practitioner who is familiar with different probiotic and prebiotic combinations that make up the psychobiotic.

While their benefits are greatly positive, you need to make sure that you do not get ahead of yourself by overloading your system. Know that the bacteria work very quickly and it is very condensed, so you do not need to aim for large amounts in order to feel the positive impacts. Allow yourself to get used to the way that they are going to work for you, being mindful that you can always adjust this in the future, if necessary. You can typically obtain your psychobiotics in pill form. This tends to be one of the easiest ways to consume them. Again, work with a practitioner who is familiar with prescribing and monitoring the use of psychobiotics.

The same standard recommendations apply while taking psychobiotics:

- It is preferable to take them in the morning in an effort to regulate your digestive system. Plus, this is going to create a habit that you can easily manage and you won't be as likely to forget taking them.
- Take them before you eat food so that they can work their way through your system as the food digests.
- Make sure that you take them on a daily basis so that you are able to experience their full benefits. If you stop them and start them again, your body isn't going to process them correctly, potentially resulting in no noticeable changes to your bodily functions.
- Be sure to pay attention to the way that you feel, as your instincts are going to guide you along the way during this process. You should know when your stomach feels right and your mood is stable. If you notice any negative changes in either of these things, make sure that you monitor your dosage carefully.

There are some companies that actually make foods that are infused with psychobiotics for your consumption. This allows you to get your psychobiotics while simultaneously giving you your prebiotic fiber, as well. While this can be a great source of psychobiotics and an easy way to consume them, this kind of food is not readily available all around the country. If you have the advantage of living near a health food store, you might be able to find psychobiotics this way. Do your research and make sure that you are utilizing all of your resources.

If you prefer to take your psychobiotics in a powder form, you can use this instead of pills. This does require you to mix the powder into your meal or your beverage, though. It can be a little bit more difficult to remember to take them this way when you have the option of taking a single pill instead. If you want, you can give each one a try to see which one best fits with your current lifestyle. Both are going to provide you with the same amount of psychobiotics that you need in order to feel a positive difference.

The Future of Psychobiotics

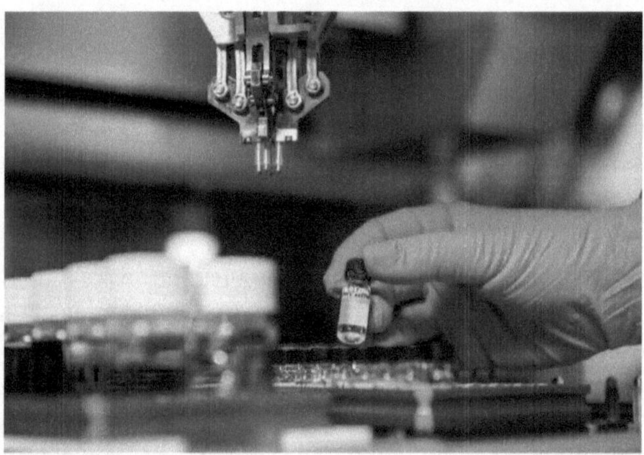

Research continues on the efficacy of psychobiotics.

Because the discovery of psychobiotics is fairly new, there are many studies that are still currently taking place regarding their effectiveness. Just one decade ago, it was seen as unlikely that bacteria in your gut could impact the way that your body could actually guide your mental health and your behavior.

Faith Dickerson, PhD, MPH, is a clinical psychologist at the Sheppard Pratt Health System in Baltimore, MD. She studies infectious and immune factors in mental illness. Because of her role in the health care system, naturally, psychobiotics have caught her attention. In the last several years, Pratt has seen some very compelling evidence that supports just how comprehensive the gut microbiome can be for the second brain as well as the first.

While it is known that the gut and the main brain communicate on a regular basis, scientists are still amazed at how exactly this works — this is what they are still aiming to unravel. Most scientists are actually in awe of the system because it is so intricate and effective, with seemingly no help from any outside factors. They just work together and they work well. Despite the complexity of the situation, this only drives scientists to work harder to discover more answers about the endless questions that have surfaced. They are doing testing that will hopefully shed some light on the process and break down the aspects that are involved.

Many scientists have already come to the same conclusion that gut problems will often go hand-in-hand with mental health problems. They know that it is no coincidence that one will often follow the other. As discussed in a prior chapter, these symptoms tend to follow one another because of the way that your body communicates to its various systems. Going off of this notion, research has shown that those who have gastrointestinal disorders also have higher than average rates of neuropsychiatric disorders. These include bipolar disorder and schizophrenia. Something that these individuals who have both share in common are that there is inflammation present in the gut. As you know, inflammation can trigger diseases and even make them worse. This serves as proof of just how much gut inflammation can impact your main brain.

Since studies have been taking place, researchers have come to some conclusions about the patterns that have been discovered. Christopher Lowry, PhD, associate professor of integrative psychology at the University of Colorado Boulder, states that the gut and the microbiome communicate with the brain. This communication does not end there, however, because the brain is also communicating back to the gut and microbiome. This is a steady, two-way communication that has a lot of different implications.

So far, a few conclusions have been made. Lowry explains that one reason could be the way that communication between the two brains works. One idea is that messages travel through the digestive tract to the brain along the vagus nerve. This creates a highway of sorts that extends from the gut to the brainstem. Because the groundwork is already there naturally, this serves as an excellent and direct track for this communication. Based on this finding, your current mental health is going to have a lot to do with the effectiveness of the way that these messages travel. If your brain chemistry is abnormal, the highway might not be clear to create a direct path for these messages. This can lead to inflammation and the worsening of any illnesses that you might be experiencing.

Another study has uncovered evidence that supports the idea of the gut generating metabolites that circulate through your blood that then flow into your brain. This idea also makes sense because that is how a lot of other organisms travel. The blood stream is a quick and easy way to ensure that they are going through all of the most important systems in your body. It is fascinating to imagine because your brain isn't exactly telling your gut to create these metabolites; it just simply knows what to do out of an instinctual need. Through this process, it is likely able to maintain successful communication that helps us function on a daily basis.

Lowry has expanded on this research by creating more studies done on mice and stress-related pathologies. In the study, researchers housed mice in colonies, with one dominant aggressor per colony. Normally, subordinate mice show signs of anxiety and end up developing colitis (or inflammation of the colon) as a result of it — a clear indication of the gut-brain connection. To further the study, researchers injected some of the mice with heat-killed bacteria known as Mycobacterium vaccae. In previous research, this bacteria was shown to eliminate inflammation inside the body. Much like creating a vaccine via psychobiotics, the researchers saw positive results with the mice. They were better able to handle the stressor (the aggressive mouse) without developing gut-related responses.

A week after experiencing this treatment, the mice who had been injected with the strain of good bacteria showed lower levels of inflammation. Compared to the control mice, Lowry reported that these mice also no longer showed as many submissive behaviors. Therefore, there was much less anxiety and fear present. The makeshift vaccine was able to control both gut functions and mental functions. They also expanded on the study by placing the mice through a difficult maze. The mice with the good bacteria were able to navigate it without giving in to stress or fear.

Overall, the initial studies that are being done on psychobiotics are proving to yield promising results. With more studies, researchers should have many of the answers that they are looking for in the near future; about how psychobiotics can significantly improve similar conditions in humans.

Chapter 10: Taking Action

Accomplishment is a great motivator. What are the next steps toward overall health that you need to take?

Now that you have all of this information to work with regarding your gut health, you should be able to make changes in your own life that will reflect what you have learned. It does not take a lot to ensure that you are paying close attention to your gut health. Whether you try all of the tips or only some of them, you should be able to notice real improvements in the way that your body and mind are able to function. Through a detailed and step-by-step approach, you will be able to improve your ailments and maintain steady communication between your gut and your main brain.

Diet and Exercise

Whether you have an illness that you would like to better control or if you are worried about developing one, you can rest assured that maintaining your gut health is a very proactive step that you can take. Start by doing an assessment of your current health, making sure that you closely observe the way that you are eating and sleeping. As yourself questions like...

How active is your lifestyle?

Do you find that you have enough energy to complete all of the tasks that you are presented with throughout the day?

How do you feel after meals? Energized or sleepy?

These little hints are going to tell you a lot about the overall picture of your health.

Once you discover the areas that could use some work, ask yourself what you can do differently. Are you able to change your diet to incorporate more nutritious food? Can you exercise more frequently and go to sleep a little bit earlier? Most people can, so it all comes down to a matter of actually wanting to. These small steps are going to amount to bigger results the more that you practice them. Make a commitment to creating small changes in each aspect of your life. When you notice that you are feeling better, make sure that you determine what is helping you to feel this way.

Make sure that you are eating plenty of foods that contain high vitamin and nutrient content. If you want to do this effectively, it makes sense to place yourself on a diet that will provide you with some kind of structure. As seen in the earlier chapters of this book, you do not necessarily need to give up on eating the foods that you love for the sake of improving your gut health. You can, however, aim to incorporate more healthy foods into the diet that you already maintain. It shouldn't be difficult when you are able to remember that consuming these foods will end up helping you in more ways than one.

If you do decide to completely change your diet, you don't have to subject yourself to a strict routine. Go with one that already closely resembles the way that you eat. When you do this, you are giving yourself a better chance of being able to transition into it rather than creating a shock through your system. Aim to eat foods that will allow you to function well and that will promote a healthy gut. When you know just how important this system is to your body, you should be able to do your own research in order to figure out what is going to work for you.

Keep your body moving. Through all of the research that you have read so far, it is notably a pattern that the human body will forget how to do certain things the longer that it remains stagnant. Not only will skills be forgotten, but endurance will also be impacted. Start out slowly, just as you will when you begin your new diet. Recognize how great you feel in every part of your body when you commit to getting active. Acknowledge how your mental health is also going to be impacted by this.

The key to preventing many diseases such as IBS and Alzheimer's comes from the way that you are able to exercise your body and, in turn, your brain. A healthy digestive system is going to keep your stomach happy and free from inflammation in order to avoid worsening your IBS, while working on various aspects of your gut health can actually improve your brain's memory function in an effort to avoid the worsening of

Alzheimer's. Everything is interconnected and your efforts matter. The more actionable steps that you take to improve your daily lifestyle, the better results you will see.

Using Prebiotics and Probiotics

After reading about all of the great things that prebiotics and probiotics can do for you, it is likely that you want to start taking them. This is one of the best actionable steps that you can take while hoping to improve your gut health. Because it is so easy, you will likely be able to effortlessly incorporate these two factors into your daily routine. Although it has been said how both prebiotics and probiotics are great for your system and essential for allowing your body to function well, there are many different kinds to choose from. It is recommended that you still complete your own research in an effort to seek out the best ones for you. Work with a healthcare practitioner, if needed.

Remember, more is not always better. It is much better to start with a lower dose prebiotic and probiotic; it might be all you need. Quality supplements can be found in most natural health stores. Because they are sensitive to heat, it's best to purchase supplements that are cold shipped and stored in a refrigerated section of the store. Also, make sure to check the guarantee that live cultures are present. Some brands are much better than others, and you do pay more for quality. But, in the long run, a better brand will be much more effective.

Fasting for Gut Health

Another great way that you can take action is by fasting. This is something that requires a lot of commitment and effort, so make sure that you are both mentally and physically prepared for the challenge. While there are certain types of fasting that are suitable for beginners, it is going to be difficult during some stages because it is probably new for you. This is expected and normal. Do not let the idea of the unknown keep you from potentially improving your gut health in a big way. Remember the underlying principle that surrounds the idea of fasting — it is done to help your body reset itself, not to starve yourself until you lose weight.

IMPORTANT NOTE: If you have a history of eating disorders, a fast is not recommended. There are other ways, as we've discussed, to improve the health of your second brain without triggering negative behaviors. Focus on the other strategies outlined, including general good eating, exercise and supplementation, as well as stress management. Skip the fast.

If you choose to fast, the fast itself is only the very first step. What you do after you fast is just as important, if not more so. Keeping the various diets that you have learned about in mind, create a plan for yourself for what you might eat after you finish with one of your fasting periods. Know that you do not have to be entirely strict with yourself, but you must have self-discipline. Eating a lot at once is not going to allow your body to have a chance to adjust back into consuming whole foods. Be easy on yourself and go slowly. It is much better to be overly cautious than to overwhelm yourself.

Stress Management

We've talked about how stress contributes to poor gut health, and vice versa. So, let's explore that just a little bit more.

When you are under stress, be it short or long-term, your body acts physically to protect itself and prepare for an impending "attack." This is the proverbial saber-tooth tiger response. Your body readies itself to protect against any injuries by triggering the inflammation response, which is great for moving blood to a wound. Your body also knows that you might need to fight or run, so blood moves away from non-vital functions, like digestion, to vital functions; like your brain, heart and lungs. During the stress response, blood also flows to your limbs, to give your muscles strength to fight or flee.

All of this is great if it's just a short-term threat - like a saber-tooth tiger. But the reality is that most of us never face an actual physical threat. Most of our stress response is due to emotional, or "imaginary" stress. But, the body doesn't know the difference between the feeling of stress from a saber-tooth tiger, or the feeling of stress because you can't make the mortgage payment. It reacts the same way - the "fight or flight" response.

Again, in the short-term, say 20-30 minutes, this is no big deal. But, when it continues for hours, days, weeks, months or years, we are putting our gut health at risk, as well as our overall health, since the stress response is meant to be very short lasting. Being on alert, all the time, means that our digestive system isn't getting the blood flow it needs, and everything else is overstimulated.

The best way to counter this is by initiating the opposite of the stress response. That is, to deliberately initiate the relaxation response.

The relaxation response is the exact opposite of the stress response. Blood flows back to the digestive system, breathing relaxes, blood pressure normalizes, and the inflammatory process calms itself.

There are several ways to do this - basically, by doing things that relax you naturally (not by substance). For example:

- Reading a book
- Drawing or painting
- Meditation
- Taking a walk
- Yoga
- Deep breathing
- Exercise

Managing your stress, by practicing the relaxation response, is one of the best ways you can calm your body, and make sure your second and first brain are getting the oxygen and nutrients they need. You'll be literally reversing inflammation in the body, and regulating your cardiovascular as well as your digestive systems. This brings balance to your immune system, as well.

Take just 10-15 minutes a day relaxing - deliberately. Watch your breathing, pay attention to your heart rate, and relax your muscles. Clear your mind, and let negative thoughts pass through your mind. Hypnotherapy can also be helpful, as well as guided meditations. You can find resources on mindful meditations online, including recorded sessions that can help you learn these simple techniques to bring balance to your life.

Conclusion

The human body is a complex system and even top scientists are still doing research to learn more about it to this day. Everyone needs to eat to survive and everyone needs to have a functioning digestive system that is going to take the food that is consumed and turn it into nourishment. By placing a priority on your gut health, you are protecting your second brain.

Because of the way that the two brains communicate with one another, it is never a bad idea to do what you can to help ensure that this stream of communication stays steady. By taking the advice given in this guide, you can perform actionable steps that will not only improve the way that your body functions but also the way that you feel. Stressors impact everyone at any given time, but you no longer have to let them rule over you. Imagine how much better your life will be when you have a functioning digestive system and a clear head to work with.

There are no shortcuts to achieving optimal health. The usual formula applies - eat well, exercise, and manage your stress. Along with these basics, taking effective prebiotic and probiotic supplements can help increase your overall health as well as your emotional health.

By paying attention to your gut health, or your second brain, you can affect your general health. Every system in the body is connected, so in some ways, it's no surprise that there is a connection between your second brain health and how the rest of your physiological systems function. Just as your second and first brain are always communicating with each other, take the time to communicate back; primarily by listening and taking positive action.

What does your body tell you? Are you generally tired, or energetic? Is your skin healthy? Does your digestive system work well or poorly? Are your emotions generally positive or negative? How is your weight - do you feel it's healthy, or do you feel bloated and inflamed? All of these symptoms and signs are speaking to you. If you pay attention to your gut health, all of these systems can normalize and balance.

Your second brain is speaking to you. Are you listening?

What did you think of 'Your second brain'?

First of all we just wanted to thank you for choosing our book and we really hope it has impacted your life in a positive way. We create our books with our customers in mind, finding solutions to their problems and hopefully changing their lives for the better.

If we have made a positive influence on you or if you have found some benefit from our book it would be greatly appreciate if you could share our book to your family and friends by posting it on your social media like Facebook and Instagram. It could make a positive impact on many other people lives.

If you liked our book why not tell others and leave a review on amazon. We would love to hear what you think and your support will help us greatly by pushing our book to more people.

If you want to just give us feedback on how we can improve our book, please just contact us on our social media we would love to hear from you and your feedback will help us make our books even better.

We want you, the reader to know we greatly appreciate you and your reviews, feedback and support is very important to us.

We wish you all the best in your future success!

Copy this link to leave a review - https://amzn.to/333zpKL

STOP!

YOU'RE PROBABLY GOING TO WANT TO READ THIS BEFORE GOING ANY FURTHER!

How would you like to enjoy our books for free?

And

Have influence on the creation of our books like covers, chapters and more...

Well you can and it's pretty simple, you can join our reader's circle and as well as get the benefits above you will get book recommendations, tips and advice from others in our amazing circle.

If you want to join our reader circle copy the link below into a web browser

https://bit.ly/READERSCIRCLE

A FREE GIFT!

As a thank you for purchasing this Book we have decided to give away a free gift. The gift we have decided to give is a 2 week meal plan which will heal and restore your gut and microbiome to optimal health.

This meal plan has a variety of tasty and easy to make recipes and I am confident you will love being on this diet. I and my team have personally engaged in this diet found the food to be delicious and the diet satisfying and easy to maintain.

Just copy the text below into a web browser

to get this guide

https://bit.ly/secondbrain2

We have also included 17 amazingly tasty recipes you can try.

Take action to a healthier, happier and tastier life.

Just copy the text below for our yummy meal plan!

https://bit.ly/secondbrain2

References

Adaes, S. (2018, July 2). What is Glutamate? Retrieved from https://neurohacker.com/what-is-glutamate

Bolen, B. (2019, July 1). Are Bacteria in Your Stomach Behind Your Irritable Bowel Syndrome? Retrieved from https://www.verywellhealth.com/gut-bacteria-and-ibs-1945285

Carpenter, S. (2012, September). That gut feeling. Retrieved from https://www.apa.org/monitor/2012/09/gut-feeling

Eske, J. (2019, August 19). Dopamine vs. serotonin: Similarities, differences, and relationship. Retrieved from https://www.medicalnewstoday.com/articles/326090

Food Insight. (2018, October 10). Everything You Need To Know About Glutamate And Monosodium Glutamate. Retrieved from https://foodinsight.org/everything-you-need-to-know-about-glutamate-and-monosodium-glutamate/

Foster, J. A. (2013, July 1). Gut feelings: bacteria and the brain. Retrieved from https://www.ncbi.nlm.nih.gov/pmc/articles/PMC3788166/

Ghannoum, M. (2020, January 28). How Intermittent Fasting Affects Your Microbiome. Retrieved from https://www.cleanplates.com/eat/tips-eat/intermittent-fasting-affects-microbiome/

Hadhazy, A. (2010, February 12). Think Twice: How the Gut's "Second Brain" Influences Mood and Well-Being. Retrieved from https://www.scientificamerican.com/article/gut-second-brain/

Harvard Health Publishing. (2015, August). DASH or Mediterranean: Which diet is better for you? Retrieved from https://www.health.harvard.edu/diet-and-weight-loss/dash-or-mediterranean-which-diet-is-better-for-you

Harvard Health Publishing. (2018, August). Are gut bacteria linked to heart health? Retrieved from https://www.health.harvard.edu/staying-healthy/are-gut-bacteria-linked-to-heart-health

Hilton-Andersen, C. (2020, February 13). Is Fasting Good for Your Gut Bacteria? Retrieved from https://www.shape.com/healthy-eating/diet-tips/benefits-of-fasting-gut-health

LoveBug Probiotics. (2019, April 8). 13 Foods to Avoid to Support a Good Gut Health Diet. Retrieved from https://www.lovebugprobiotics.com/13-foods-that-are-terrible-for-your-gut-health/

LoveBug Probiotics. (2019, September 6). When's the Best Time to Take Probiotics and Why. Retrieved from https://www.lovebugprobiotics.com/probiotics-101-whens-the-best-time-to-take-probiotics/

Michelon, P. (2019, October 19). What are Cognitive Abilities and Skills, and How to Boost Them? Retrieved from https://sharpbrains.com/blog/2006/12/18/what-are-cognitive-abilities/

Moore, M. (2019, May 3). What Are Prebiotics? Retrieved from https://health.usnews.com/health-news/blogs/eat-run/articles/what-are-prebiotics

Nutritional Requirements throughout the Life Cycle: Nutrition Guide for Clinicians. (2018, January 12). Retrieved from https://nutritionguide.pcrm.org/nutritionguide/view/Nutrition_Guide_for_Clinicians/1342043/all/Nutritional_Requirements_throughout_the_Life_Cycle#4

Prebiotics vs Probiotics: What are the key differences & health benefits. (n.d.). Retrieved from https://www.prebiotin.com/prebiotin-academy/what-are-prebiotics/prebiotics-vs-probiotics/

Ramsay Health Care. (n.d.). Intestinal bacteria could accelerate Alzheimer's. Retrieved from https://www.ramsayhealth.co.uk/about/latest-news/gut-bacteria-alzheimers

Robertson, R. (2017, June 27). Why the Gut Microbiome is Crucial for Your Health. Retrieved from https://www.healthline.com/nutrition/gut-microbiome-and-health#section2

Scottcha. (2017, September 27). Retrieved from http://psychobiotic-revolution.com/2017/09/what-are-psychobiotics/

'Second brain' neurons keep colon moving. (2018, May 29). Retrieved from https://www.sciencedaily.com/releases/2018/05/180529132122.htm

Spritzler, F. (2019, April 12). 21 Reasons to Eat Real Food. Retrieved from https://www.healthline.com/nutrition/21-reasons-to-eat-real-food#section1

Stewart, L. (2019, August 20). What's the link between the brain, stress and the gut microbiome? Retrieved from https://atlasbiomed.com/blog/stress-anxiety-depression-microbiome/

Svoboda, E. (2020, January 29). Could the gut microbiome be linked to autism?
    Retrieved from https://www.nature.com/articles/d41586-020-00198-y

The Brain-Gut Connection. (n.d.). Retrieved from
    https://www.hopkinsmedicine.org/health/wellness-and-prevention/the-brain-
    gut-connection

Water Fasting (Benefits & How to Break the Fast) I The LifeCo. (2020, February 4).
    Retrieved from https://www.thelifeco.com/en/blog/common-questions-about-
    water-fasting-benefits-how-to-break-the-fast/

Weir, K. (12AD). The future of psychobiotics. Retrieved from
    https://www.apa.org/monitor/2018/12/cover-psychobiotics

Image Sources

Accomplishment (n.d.). Retrieved from https://unsplash.com/photos/1tFd-Bb1pxk

Brain (n.d.). Retrieved from https://unsplash.com/photos/so1L3jsdD3Y

Depression (n.d.). Retrieved from https://unsplash.com/photos/IqSaG9zv2eo

Diet (n.d.). Retrieved from https://unsplash.com/photos/GiIiRVoFjwU

Emotion (n.d.). Retrieved from https://unsplash.com/photos/iprSslEBheg

Food (n.d.). Retrieved from https://unsplash.com/photos/4_jhDO54BYg

Germs (n.d.). Retrieved from https://unsplash.com/photos/UTPySVmQAco

Glass of Water (n.d.). Retrieved from https://unsplash.com/photos/7b1W1mcwekw

Head (n.d.). Retrieved from https://unsplash.com/photos/WCPg9ROZbMo

Health (n.d.). Retrieved from https://unsplash.com/photos/tb5A-QTI6xg

Illness (n.d.). Retrieved from https://unsplash.com/photos/yoo1Z-9HQAw

Lightbulbs (n.d.). Retrieved from https://unsplash.com/photos/CM-qccHaQo4

Microscope (n.d.). Retrieved from https://unsplash.com/photos/WsYamymQIxk

Probiotics (n.d.). Retrieved from https://unsplash.com/photos/lXMPY-xzMNU

Research (n.d.). Retrieved from https://unsplash.com/photos/9kSTF9PvETM

Science (n.d.). Retrieved from https://unsplash.com/photos/L9EV3OogLho

Shots (n.d.). Retrieved from https://unsplash.com/photos/2bGL3ydxJzs

Video Game (n.d.). Retrieved from https://unsplash.com/photos/NmCQdnw1Aio

Glossary

Word	Meaning
Dopamine	A chemical that your body makes to send messages between nerve cells.
GABA	Gamma-aminobutyric acid; an inhibitory acid that prevents certain parts of your brain from taking action.
Glutamate	An amino acid that signals certain parts of your brain to take action.
IBS	Irritable bowel syndrome; a disorder that causes stomach pain, gas, diarrhea, and constipation.
MSG	Monosodium glutamate; the salt that comes from glutamate.
Neuron	A nerve cell that makes up for a building block of the nervous system.
Neurotransmitter	Chemical messengers that transmit signals across your body.
Serotonin	A feel-good chemical transmitter that can make you happy.
SSRIs	Selective serotonin uptake inhibitor; a medication that can be used to treat depression.